'9

Knock

An Illustrated and Spoken history of Knock, East Belfast

by

Aidan Campbell

First published in the United Kingdom, 2008, by Aidan Campbell
Copyright Aidan Campbell
Printed by Priory Press, Holywood, Co.Down.

ISBN 978-0-9558152-0-1

Our address & phone are:
1 Inverary Fold
Inverleith drive
BELFAST
BT4 1SU
028 9065 4457

To John
On your 90th birthday
Best wishes
Kate & John

To the following for their generous contribution towards printing and publishing costs:
Gerry McKernan and friends. Stan and Sylvia Tracey and friends.
John Doyle (formerly of Owen Varra), John McClelland and Pat Leneghan,

Contents

Dedication

To some 'Marie Curie Friends'

Raymond Craig, Margaret Edgar, Paddy Morrow,
Mo Allen and Walter Munn

James Ch.4 v 13

'For what is your life? It is even a vapour, that appeareth for a little time, and then vanisheth away'

A special mention

For the staff and volunteers who daily provide a warm welcome at reception, good food in the kitchen, service with a smile on the wards and generally keep the Marie Curie Hospice, Belfast clean, tidy, friendly and welcoming for the patients and their visitors.

All proceeds from the sale of this book go to the Marie Curie Hospice, Belfast.

Thanks to everyone who bought a copy of *Beaconsfield,* sold a copy, organised a book talk, listened to the talk or contributed in any way.

There is a third book on the way. It will be called *Cherryvalley* and will be out in the spring of 2009.

About this Book

The Marie Curie Centre, Belfast celebrated its 40th birthday in August 2005.

By a coincidence the 40th birthday is also the anniversary of my 5th year as a volunteer at the Marie Curie Hospice. My work as a volunteer is mainly concerned with serving meals to the patients and washing the dishes at Marie Curie on a Thursday afternoon with Vicky and on a Sunday morning with Jill.

I also volunteered to write a history of the Marie Curie Hospice (originally known as Beaconfield Nursing Home and then Marie Curie Centre until the name change in July 2006) and Knock District. This was published in June 2005 just prior to the birthday celebrations under the title of *"Beaconsfield"*. My purpose in writing *Beaconsfield* was to raise funds for the capital appeal (£3.5m) to build a new extension at the Hospice. The extension was completed and opened for business in July 2006 although the fund-raising continues under the heading of "Living Rooms Appeal". The original print run for *Beaconsfield* was 1,000 copies and I am pleased to report that this batch of books is almost sold out. I gained valuable sponsorship support for printing costs from Michael Lorimer at Henderson Foodservice, Mallusk and from Stan and Sylvia Tracey who organised a very successful barn dance. This generosity meant that when the books were eventually sold – 100% of the proceeds from the sale of each book went directly to the Living Rooms Appeal.

The books were sold either at the Hospice reception or through the generosity of a network of friends and neighbours or via illustrated talks about *Beaconsfield* which I gave with slideshow to local church, social and history groups. I have completed and enjoyed delivering around 40 talks to local groups and on each occasion sold many copies of the book.

The *Beaconsfield* talks were great fun. The slideshows brought back many happy memories to my audience – and some sad ones too – from long ago and how things used to be before the present rush to change everything. I noticed that many of the people at the talks were of senior years and actually remembered the events and people that I talked about – and in fact they knew lots of things of which I was unaware.

On the left is an autumn scene in September 2005 as the foundations for the new extension at the Marie Curie Centre are laid and on the right a more summery scene showing the completed building in August 2006.

The original Beaconfield Nursing Home had cost £120,000 in 1965 and the aim of the Living Rooms Appeal in 2005 was to raise £3.5m for the new extension. Notice the side view of Owen Varra at 60 Knock Road in the background of both photos

Often reminiscence would begin with: "I remember…"

The memory may have been an event such as The Second World War; an old house now demolished; the village feel of the Knock area before the various road-widening schemes; an old shop; attendance at an old school; a local hero; the railway line; a parent or ancestor who had lived in interesting times or even a life threatening or life changing experience.

I am amazed at the extent to which people lovingly keep and maintain family photograph collections and archives – which of course makes the whole business of writing a history book so much easier. One memory that does stick in my mind was a talk I gave to Cregagh Methodist Ladies. I was telling the story with pictures of the trams and trolleybuses that used to pass the church hall on their way from the city centre to Bell's Bridge and on to the "end-of-lines" beside the (now) House of Orange next to Cregagh Park. A lady raised her hand and said:

I remember the trams… I used to work at Station Street beside Queens Quay near the railway terminus. I took the tram to work every day …one day the tram was full up and I had to stand…. and as I looked at a young man sitting in the seat beside me…he looked at me and smiled…he stood up and gave me his seat……….I thanked him and sat down……….we got married and had 50 happy years together…he died just last year….

With each talk I began to gather up more anecdotes and stories and then it struck me: I need to volunteer and write another book before all this wonderful material is forgotten or lost forever!

This book is slightly more expansive in terms of geographical area than *Beaconsfield* (there are still copies available for sale at the Marie Curie Hospice – and the talk with slideshow is available and very entertaining – telephone for details).

This time the aim is to review the history of Knock through the lens of old photographs but particularly with oral history and reminiscence. There will be some overlap with the *Beaconsfield* story although most of the material has not previously been published.

A 1930's view of a 'McCreary' Tram on the Cregagh Road at Bell's Bridge before it became a roundabout. Bell's Bridge is clearly marked on the 1858 Ordnance Survey map and is visible immediately behind the tram with the Belfast City boundary post. Horse-drawn trams travelled to the top of the Cregagh Road where it met the Hillfoot Road by 1904 and a trolleybus service replaced the electric trams in February 1941 with a turning circle at Cregagh Park.

My 'stretched' definition of Knock is to encompass the Knock Road from the Upper Newtownards Road through to the old Hillfoot Road, previously known in Street Directories as the Knockbreda Road and now better known as the Upper Knockbreda Road

This story is partly a historical and factual record of the area but also includes the memories of a few of the people who lived in the area and have a story to tell. I really enjoyed hearing their everyday stories and some of their life's minutiae. Their old photos interested me greatly and I hope they enjoy seeing their lives illustrated in this book. I am sure there are lots of people in the Knock area with old photographs and long memories that I have not interviewed – maybe they would contact me, as I would like to hear their stories too.

As another great supporter of *Beaconsfield* remarked when she saw some of her family life in the narrative: '*I didn't realise that my life was so interesting to a total stranger until you told me!*'

This book probably works best as a travel guide to the architectural and social history of the Knock area and to get the best from the content why not take a walk and spot the places mentioned – or at least in your imagination as many buildings have disappeared forever.

I am available to give talks and slideshow on both books so simply ring the Marie Curie Hospice at 028 90 882000 to arrange a booking. As previously, thanks to everybody who helped make *Beaconsfield* a resounding success. All proceeds from book sales and talk fees go to the Marie Curie Hospice, Kensington Road, Belfast.

Any oversights or mistakes in the telling of *Knock* are all down to the storyteller.

Marie Curie Cancer Care was formed in 1948 as The Marie Curie Memorial Foundation and celebrates 60 years of age in 2008.

Aidan Campbell
November 2007

Origins of Knock District

To start our story we first have to describe where Knock is located. Knock is not an easy area to define. It is not an electoral district although since 1896 St Columba's church does provide a more recent parish boundary. According to old maps Knock is a townland and it is also the name of a small river. At its extremes, Knock Fire Station is on the Upper Newtownards Road beside North Road, Knock Golf Club is at Stormont facing Dundonald Cemetery and Knock Road travels from the Upper Newtownards Road to Castlereagh.

John Auld of the East Belfast Historical Society noted that: *Past researches have indicated that prehistoric man lived in the (Knock) area around the mound in Shandon Park previously called Dundela and we know that there was a track which came from the Lagan Valley along the line of the Upper Knockbreda dual carriageway (or Hillfoot Road) via the Old Dundonald Road (now King's Road) and through the Dundonald Gap. The reason is simple, to go further along the River Lagan meant swampy land and to go right meant hills so the more level and dry passage was used. In the 12th Century the Normans built a motte at Shandon Park at one end of a high ridge that crosses the Knock dual carriageway and at the other end a church (at Knockmount Park) with a great view of Lagan Valley and the Dundonald Gap.*

H.Crawford Miller painted an interesting picture of life at Castlereagh and Gilnahirk during the late 1700's in his book 'The Church on the Stye Brae': *The people lived in a dark world lit only by candles and oil lamps. Life was harsh, being full of trials and tribulations, and death was a constant companion. Disease and fever ravaged all, especially the young, whose mortality rate was so high that two children in five would have been fortunate to reach the age of ten; hence large families were common in an effort to ensure that at least a few of the offspring would survive. Rarely did anyone travel further than a ten mile radius from their home; this was approximately the distance one could walk from home, do a day's work and return home again in the evening.*

The ordinary working folk had little time or money for entertainment. A cup of tea and a chat with a few neighbours by the fireside would have been enjoyed every bit as much as an elaborate modern show. The latest news would have been obtained in such places as the market or the Church where people came together.

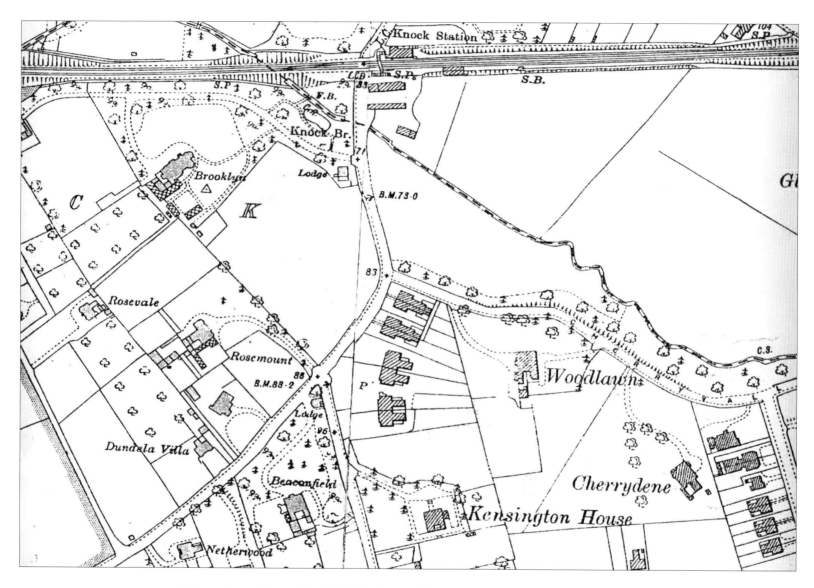

(Reproduced from the 1920 Ordnance Survey of Northern Ireland Map)

The Ordnance Map of Knock Road for 1920. Most of the houses named have been demolished.

Peddlers and journeymen such as tailors and tinsmiths were also a source of information, for they related what was 'going on' as they travelled from farm to farm and district to district. Ministers travelled a lot throughout their congregations, sometimes on horseback, comforting the dying and administering communion to the household and almost all baptisms took place in the warmth of the family home.

More recently, the Ordnance Survey Memoirs of Ireland, 1837 include a chapter for parishes which include or border on Knock such as Knockbreda, Dundonald and Comber. This provides a glimpse of life in the area during the 1830's.

The Donaghadee mail car passes through the village of Dundonald (and past Knock Road) at about 9.30am to Donaghadee from Belfast, but its return is uncertain on account of the packet (ship). Coaches from Portaferry and Comber pass through the village every morning to Belfast and return in the evening. The mail coach road runs across the parish in its greatest breadth dividing it nearly in half. The road is repaired by the county but is kept very badly.

The parish of Knockbreda is bounded on the north by Belfast Lough, on the east by the parishes of Dundonald and Comber, on the south by the parish of Drumbo and on the west by the River Lagan. Its greatest length from north to south is nearly five miles and its greatest breadth from east to west is about four miles. The soil is clay from which bricks are made and when these bricks cannot be disposed of in the town of Belfast they are often sent out as ballast in vessels going to the West Indies. The roads are now tolerably well laid out (in Castlereagh) considering improvements having lately been made in them. They are not kept in good repair and even the high road to Donaghadee is in a very bad state owing to not having people constantly on them to fill up the holes.

The inhabitants of this part of Ireland are half Scotch in their language and manners. Their religion is generally of the Presbyterian and there are several meeting houses in the parish. They are generally well educated, that is, they can read and write. Their food is generally potatoes and oatmeal. Their fuel is generally coal which is imported from Scotland and Wales, there being no bog in the parish of any consequence. Coals are from 13 shillings (65p) to £1 per ton.

In the townland of Knock the school master receives £25 a year from the children and £7 and 10 shillings from a subscription. The ruins of Knock Church are in the same townland and but a portion of the ruins remain to show that the building was not at any time extensive. There is but one more small school (in Castlereagh) comprising two boys and six girls, taught by an old man merely for his own amusement and to occupy his leisure hours. He receives 2d per week from each scholar. It is under no society nor patronised by no one.

The Ordnance Survey of Northern Ireland keep a document entitled 'Co Down Name Book, Sheet 4.' This is an old handwritten ledger containing an archive or index of the names of roads, localities, residential, business and public buildings contained within Sheet 4 of the Ordnance Survey map for the area, which includes Knock. In handwritten script the book records that the names were collected and entered initially by a team of three people. In April 1902 the Name Book team included: William Summerhayes, J.Pratley, and W.H.Gregg.

It looks like this team actually walked around the area to discover and record the names of buildings and places and the names of the occupier or householder. They also recorded a brief description of the area. It was the practice also to record the name of a person in authority who could validate or stand over the name as the correct title in use. Suitable authority figures were for example such dignitaries as the Belfast City Surveyor, a solicitor, a local clergyman or the postmaster.

The Belfast Street Directory reflects the custom that residences and other buildings did not have numbers but only names for postal and other identification purposes. It was in the 1930's that numbers were introduced to households in the Knock district and in fact as late as the 1950's some houses such as Beaconsfield, Brooklyn and The Orchard were known only by their names.

The earliest Ordnance Survey of Northern Ireland to include Knock was the 1834 map surveyed by Captain English and Lieutenants Bordes and Tucker, Royal Engineers under the direction of the Ordnance Survey Office, Phoenix Park, Dublin and revised in 1858 by Captain Wilkinson. The 1858 map shows the Knock area beginning to take shape although Knock is clearly a rural setting with very few of the buildings and other landmarks which are recognisable today.

(Courtesy of H.Crawford Miller from an old postcard)

There are lots of trees in this view of Knock crossroads in 1920 looking right along Hawthornden Road and left towards Wandsworth Road. The large house, centre has been demolished and on the site is now a block of modern apartments. The tramlines were extended beyond Knock Depot some time after electrification in 1905 to the 'end -of -lines' at Rosepark.

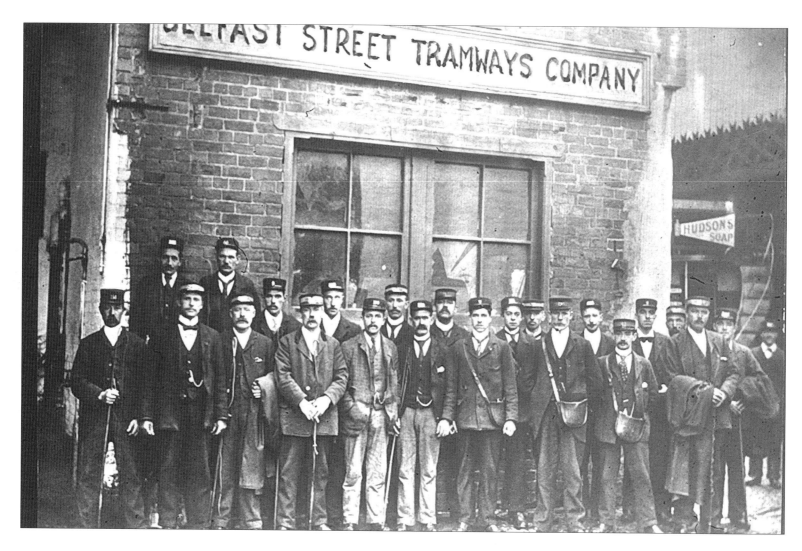

Drivers and conductors of horse-drawn trams at Belfast Street Tramways Company, Knock Depot which in 1900 was a terminus and stables. It had started out as a home for sick horses. An overnight billet for tramway men was located in a row of cottages on Wandsworth Road.

(Courtesy of Desmond Coakham)

A view of the entrance gates to Knock Tramway Depot in 1947 (demolished in 2005). When the Connswater Bridge was widened in 1890 and the Belfast City Boundary later extended to the East Belfast suburbs, the tram lines passed beyond the Holywood Arches to Knock. In 1904 Belfast Corporation had compulsorily acquired the tramway system.

A 2005 view of the Knock Road and the present Knock Methodist Church remains virtually unchanged since completion in 1883. The junction now has many lanes. To accommodate the increased road width nearly all the houses on the left hand side of the Knock Road from the Upper Newtownards Road to Glen Road at the Braniel Estate have been demolished.

In 1868 the Village Directory describes the area as 'The Knock' and there are only 30 householders recorded as living in the whole area encompassing such familiar names as Summerfield, Rosepark, Thornhill, Cabinhill and Glenview and Caseldona at Castlereagh

Knock is described in the 1902 Ordnance Survey Northern Ireland Co Down Name Book.

Various modes of Spelling	Authority for modes of Spelling	Descriptive Remarks, or other General Observations which may be considered of Interest.
Knock	*Mr M Anderson, Postmaster, Knock.*	*Knock applies to an extensive district in the eastern portion of Belfast. Bounded on the north by Belmont, west by Bloomfield and on the east by the City boundary. There is a Post Office, Railway Stations and various churches in this district. Owners various.*
Knock Road		*A road commencing on the south side of the Upper Newtownards Road immediately opposite the south end of Wandsworth Road and extending in a southerly direction to Castlereagh Road*

(Reproduced from the 1902 Ordnance Survey of Northern Ireland Name Book)

(Courtesy of Gavin Bamford from an old postcard)

Knock crossroads in the 1930's. Looking across the Upper Newtownards Road the junction is virtually unrecognisable today following numerous road-widening schemes and demolition of houses. The road far left is Wandsworth Road and right Hawthorden Road. Notice gas lamps and absence of traffic lights and road markings. On the Ordnance Survey map of 1834 there were buildings marked on the corners at the left and at the extreme right.

A later view on 24th March 1954 of the Knock Road junction, looking across the Upper Newtownards Road towards Wandsworth Road. This scene was described in the Belfast News-Letter as a 'Dangerous Belfast Intersection'. There was a suggestion by Belfast Corporation Police Committee that a roundabout be constructed at this junction instead of proposed traffic lights. The photograph was probably taken from the upstairs of 445 Upper Newtownards Road.

(Courtesy of East Belfast Historical Society)

After electrification in 1905 the tramlines were extended in a couple of stages beyond Knock Depot. They initially ended at the city boundary near to the site of present day St Molua's Church of Ireland. This view looks from (what is now) Rosepark towards Knock and the site of the Stormont Hotel. The area to the left was described in the 1902 Belfast Street Directory as 'The Low Bog'.

(Courtesy of Mike Maybin)

The tramlines were extended in 1924 to the gates of Dundonald Cemetery facing the entrance to the newly opened Knock Golf Club which had recntly moved from Shandon Park. The shop with the pointed roof had been used as a billet for military personnel during the Second World War. Harry Walker, who played football for Belfast Celtic, then later operated a newsagency here for many years. The whole site, including Robb's Garage has been demolished and replaced by a new filling station. Notice the white telephone kiosk. Knock Telephone Exchange had been installed at 78 Earlswood Road in 1911.

It is worth mentioning some of the very few named premises from the 1858 Ordnance Survey map and the occupants named in the 1868 Village Directory. A sure sign of population growth was a shop and in 1868 the Misses Clements are described as grocers. By 1870 they operate the Post Office at 'Belmont'. In 1890 the Post Master is Martin Anderson with premises close to the site of (what is now) Huston & Co, Tax Consultants at 473 Upper Newtownards Road on the corner of Cabin Hill Park.

The Belfast and County Down Railway opened for business in 1848 with a line from Belfast to Holywood. The first portion of main line through Knock passed under 'Campbell's Bridge' at the King's Road to Dundonald, Comber and Newtownards and had opened on December 30th 1850 when trains began calling at Ballycloughan Halt, Knock Road which would later be known as Knock Station. Ballycloughan Nursery extended over an area along the Knock Road from the Upper Newtownards Road including Knockdene to the King's Road and land now occupied by Towell House as far as the railway line. The Village Directory notes that Farrell Dickson & Co operated a nursery at Knock (as early as 1843) and in fact Griffith's Valuation of Tenements for 1863 records Alexander Dickson as having leased 32 acres of land in Ballycloughan from Robert E Ward of Bangor. There is a building located on the 1858 OS map at the corner of King's Road on the nursery site. The original railway station was simply a small booking office and in 1868 the Village Directory tells us that the railway station had only 'six stoppages each day' (did they mean 'stoppages?') which was an increase from the 1852 frequency of only 'two calls in the day'. The booking office was replaced by a brick building to be known as Knock Station in 1869. By 1893 a footbridge had been constructed at the Knock Road level crossing.

Next to the railway line is Knock Bridge, a small stone structure spanning Knock Road as it crossed Knock River beside Brooklyn. At the corner of Cherryvalley and Knock Road was a Corn and Logwood Mill operated by Lewis Reford as early as 1843, where a millrace ran from the Knock River to provide power. Griffith's Valuation notes a 'house, corn-mill and kiln', owned by Sir Thomas McClure, although by 1863 the premises are described as vacant. This mill also provided a venue for a Presbyterian Sabbath School before Knock Presbyterian Church was built in 1876 and later for the Church of Ireland congregation before St Columba's, King's Road was completed in 1896. Kensington Road had not yet been laid out as a thoroughfare and would first appear in the 1898 street directory as 'Knock Avenue Road'. Further along Knock Road on the left before Sandown Road was Knock Cottage at 70 Knock Road, which survived until the 1980's road-widening scheme.

James Colville was given use of the 'Old Mill' (pictured), at the corner of Cherryvalley and Knock Road, in 1870 for the purpose of a Sabbath School for local children of Presbyterian families to attend. The building also held Church services and the Congregation was described as 'very earnest'. Sir Thomas McClure owned the 'Old Mill' and would later become a benefactor and lay the foundation stone for Knock Presbyterian Church in 1875. The Church of Ireland later held services here in 1884. The Ordnance Survey Memoirs for 1832 note the existence in the townland of Knock of 'a logwood mill with a breast wheel 23 feet in diameter'. Griffith's Valuation for 1863 describes the premises as 'unoccupied'.

(Left, Courtesy of Tony Merrick by Fred Arthur Hurley)

On the left is a view of a very spic and span Knock Station as it was in 1895 looking towards Neill's Hill. The Village Directory for 1895 describes this view as 'BCDR Station and Telegraph Office, J McCluskey Station Master'. Notice the absence of advertising signage in 1895, which would proliferate at railway stations in later years. Right, in 2005 the same view looking along the Greenway, all trace of the footbridge, level crossing and station building have gone. Trains had begun calling at Ballycloughan on 30th December 1850 and the brick station building pictured replaced a temporary hut as the booking office in 1895. The main BCDR railway network was closed in 1950 after 99 years and eleven months in business.

(Left, Courtesy of Gavin Bamford from 'Lost Railways of Co Down')

On the left is a 1920's view of Knock Station (taken from what is now PSNI HQ, Brooklyn) which shows the long platform stretching to King's Road and looking towards the King's Road bridge which was known as 'Campbells Bridge'. The Station Master in 1920 was Kensington Road resident H.Carlton. The house in the distance framed by the lattice footbridge is Willowdene, 71 King's Road. On the right is the same view as it looks in 2007. The BCDR had struggled to maintain passenger numbers as early as the 1920's when road going buses and trucks became a more common and convenient form of transport for individuals and businesses.

(Courtesy of Gavin Bamford from 'Lost Railways of Co Down')

Neill's Hill Station was opened in 1890 and the view on the left looks towards the Sandown Road crossing and on to Knock Station. In 1895 the Station master was Robert Brown. The house left of the station behind the trees was known as 'Sandown', 86 Sandown Road, the home of Mr Rebbick of Harland & Wolff. Right, approaching the site of Neill's Hill Station on the Greenway in 2007. The remains of the platform are visible in the bottom right hand corner of the photo. By the date of closure in 1950 the BCDR had been struggling financially for years although its final demise was hastened by a serious rail crash at Ballymacarrett junction on January 10th 1945. There were 23 fatalities which resulted in the BCDR paying out a large compensation claim.

THIRD CLASS WEEKLY SEASON and WORKMEN'S TICKETS - · - · -

Passengers are requested to obtain their Third Class Weekly Season and Workmen's Tickets on Saturday evenings or Sundays, as, owing to pressure, it may not be possible to issue such tickets at Stations on Monday mornings.

BELFAST AND COUNTY DOWN RAILWAY

TRAIN SERVICE

FROM

31st MAY, 1948

until further notice

BY ORDER

Belfast, May, 1948

(Courtesy of John Keenan)

The BCDR '3rd Class Weekly Season and Workmen's Ticket'
By January 1950 there would be no further need for a timetable.

Close by in 1862, Thomas McClure sold '6 acres and 16 perches' of land to John Little and a semi-detached residence known as Belgrave Cottages was constructed at 66 & 68 Knock Road by 1895. The deeds show that the house was sold for £165 in 1915 and there is a right of way for 'coal, ash-pit cleansing and like purposes'. The name of Thomas McClure appears frequently in Griffith's Valuation of Tenements for 1863 in connection with some 200 acres of land in the Knock area and he apparently granted land for the building of new houses on condition they were substantial villas standing in their own grounds (Sir Thomas McClure was a tobacco merchant and Liberal MP and he sold the site of Belmont House in 1890 to allow for the building of Campbell College). There is no evidence in 1858 of the Shandon Park development (the first three houses would be built by 1898). Knock Golf Club would open in 1895 at Cherryvalley before moving to Shandon Park in 1898 and an orchard, along with two houses, is marked on the site of the entrance to Shandon Park. On the route of Sandown Road is marked the name 'Cadgers Loaney' (or 'Old Knock Road') which continues to Ballyhackamore.

At the top of the hill on the site of Knockmount Park is Knock House occupied by Daniel McLorinan. Griffith's Valuation of 1863 describes this gentleman as having leases on 54 acres of land at Knock. Knock House is one of the few buildings noted in Knock on the 1834 Ordnance Survey map and it dates back until the 1820's - it survived until 1982. Alongside is the old Knock Burial Ground with 'Knock Church in ruins.' The church of Breda was built on the land of Belvoir Park Forest and was recorded in the taxation of Pope Nicholas IV in 1302. The taxation was originated to raise money to finance the crusades. The taxation also applied to several chapels of ease attached to Breda – one of which was Dundela, Knock Collumcill now shortened simply to Knock. The Dundela or Knock Church was allowed to fall into ruin and eventually replaced by Knockbreda Parish Church in 1744 at Church Road near present day Forestside Shopping Centre.

The 1902 entry for Knock Church (in ruins) in the Co Down Name book states: *The ruins of Knock Church stand on a high hill in the graveyard near a rath of conical form. A gable and arch of the church were in good preservation till they were gradually dilapidated by parties making way for graves and tombstones. The ruins belong to the 12th century and there is now only a small portion of one of the walls remaining.* In 1863, facing the old graveyard, Griffith's notes that John and Henry Gelston occupied some 65 acres of land. John Gelston lived in a house close to the present site of Ascot Park which was described as Knock Farm and later as Eden House (demolished in the 1930's).

Extracts from the 1902 Ordnance Survey Northern Ireland Co Down Name Book, Sheet 4

Various modes of Spelling	Authority for modes of Spelling	Descriptive Remarks, or other General Observations Which may be considered of Interest.
Knock Post Office	Mr M Henderson, Postmaster, Knock.	A sub post office situated on the south side of the Upper Newtownards Road, 28 Chains (1/3 Mile) S.E. of Ormiston. This is not a Telegraph Office Property of Baroness Clanmorris, Bangor Castle
Knock Bridge	J.C.Bretland City Suyveyor, Town Hall, Belfast	A small stone bridge on the Knock Road spanning the Knock River, 3 Chains (50 Yards) South of Knock Railway Station.
Knock River		A stream formed by the junction of two streams at a point ¼ mile North West of Summerfield. It flows through Knock to Connswater.
Campbells Bridge	G. Culverwell Engineer, BCDR	Applies to a large stone structure on the County Road over the BCDR railway situated in the townland of Ballycloughan. It is kept in repair by the County

(Courtesy of Frances Gibson by Alan Seaton)

What makes this early 1980's photograph interesting requires a close look. At the far right it is possible to see the outline of a gable-end and chimneys peeping out from behind the foliage. This semi-detached terrrace dates from the 1870's when it was the home of Samuel Gelston. It was originally known as Orangefield Terrace, later as 80-82 Knock Road and now demolished.

(Courtesy of Tony Merrick by Fred Arthur Hurley)

An 1895 view of the Knock Road, which is better known today as a busy dual carriageway. Knockwood Park is now on the left and at the top of the hill are Knockmount Park and the old Knock Burial Ground.

A similar view of Knock Road in 2007. Knockwood Park, left, had been opened in 1965 and Knockmount Park at the top of the hill in 1970. Knock House occupied the site of Ascot Mews at Knockmount Park until the late 1970's and can be dated back to the first OS map of 1834.

In the old Knock burial ground at Knockmount Park there are several headstones from the 1800's with the Gelston name visible. One grave mentions Gelston of Strandtown. Gelstons's Corner at Strandtown is the junction where the Strand cinema meets the Belmont and Holywood Road. Continuing along the right hand side of the Knock Road on a site close to Knockwood Park was Knock National School (also noted on the 1834 Ordnance Survey map), which, along with the graveyard, according to Griffith's Valuation, received a rates exemption. In 1843 the teacher was William Burke and '50 scholars' attended the school. By 1863 the master received an income of £25 per year 'from the children'. Across the Knock Road the modern Glen Road was described as Carnamuck Glen. A large house with grounds on the site of the Braniel estate was the home of George Martin and called Glen View. Across the junction of the modern Ballygowan Road on the corner were substantial brickworks that were described as 'disused' in 1904. There was a house on the nearby hill named Caseldona (later Castledona) now better known as Casaeldona which is recorded in Griffith's Valuation for 1863 to have 19 acres of land and to be occupied by Hugh Jamieson. Further along the Hillfoot Road or Knockbreda Road there were very few buildings until the Cregagh (or Craigah) Road is reached and in 1858 the Cregagh Flax Works, operated by Bernard and Koch, was located on a site close to Cregagh Park.

An interesting note on the development of communications technology was that in 1863 the British and Irish Magnetic Telegraph Company were assessed to a rateable valuation of £1 in Ballyhackmore, and 10 shillings each in Dundonald and Castlereagh, presumably for the siting of telegraph poles on the parish land.

So Belfast was beginning to experience rapid growth and whereas in the 1830's it was essentially a thriving market town and commercial centre, by the 1880's it was an industrialised city. C.E.B. Brett explained in his book, 'Buildings of Belfast 1700–1914', that the development of the town (of Belfast) was given a boost by the final downfall of the precarious finances of the Donegall family. The whole estate was placed in the hands of the Incumbered Estates Court Commissioners (1850) which was a body appointed to cut through the tangle of mortgages and borrowings with which almost every estate in Ireland had become encumbered as a result of the famine. The eventual freeing of land from the control of the Donegall family had a great impact on the expansion and development of the town. It came at an important point in the history of Belfast and contributed greatly to the rapid increase in the rate of building which characterised the second half of the nineteenth century.

(Courtesy of Frances Gibson by Alan Seaton)

Knockmount Park in 1980 looking towards the old Knock Burial Ground. Ascot Mews has not yet been built and the stone wall is the remains of Knock House which was marked on the 1834 Ordnance Survey map and latterly the business premises of Craig McDowall & Co.

Gelston's Corner in 1930 (now the site of the Strand cinema) looking along Holywood Road left. The tram in the distance is outside the former Hurley family home 'Cremorne Villa' at 106 Holywood Road which was later the Vicarage of St Patrick's, Ballymacarrett and now the Job Centre. Dr Barnardo's was at No. 112 in 1920 with the wonderful telephone number: 'Knock 84'. It was destroyed by a bomb in the 1941 Blitz. In the 1920's the RUC Barracks was a few doors along. On the corner the unusually shaped medieval-looking building was Strandtown House Lodge. There are several headstones at the Knock Burial Ground with the Gelston name.

(Courtesy of Gavin Bamford from an old postcard)

A 1940's view of Gelston's Corner from the Holywood Road. The main change from the 1930 photo is the appearance of the Strand Cinema which was opened at 152 Holywood Road on December 7th 1935 by Lord Mayor, Crawford McCullagh. It is apparently the last surviving cinema (in 2007) from the 46 in use in Belfast during the Second World War. Located next to Pim's Avenue the Strand Cinema occupies the site of Strandtown House Lodge which marked the entrance to the home of Sir Gustavus Heyn of 'Headline' shipping company fame, at Strandtown House.

Belfast was a fairly unhealthy place to live. There had been rapid port expansion and trading ships brought in epidemic diseases. C.E.B. Brett also noted that the year of 1847 was marked by the outbreaks of smallpox and dysentery amongst the poor and in 1852 potato blight was still flourishing around Belfast. The outpouring of thick smoke from factory chimneystacks was also a particular pollution problem for a low-lying city surrounded by hills. Great wealth and employment would now come from activities such as shipbuilding, railways, tobacco, linen milling and the ropeworks, but industrialisation brought overcrowding and urban growth too.

Belfast Town in the 1830's covered an area of 2½ sq miles and by 1888 this had been increased to 23 square miles and city status was granted. In fact the population of Belfast had grown from 53,000 in 1831 to 350,000 in 1901. Following the break-up of many great estates after the famine, as the High Victorian era (1867-1900) dawned, the Knock area, along with the other suburban areas of Belfast, such as Malone, began to experience residential development mainly for the burgeoning middle classes who were moving away from Belfast city centre locations where their houses were replaced by department stores. They were seeking fresh air and escape from bad smells and the throng of inner city life.

Mobility was increasing too. The coaching era was coming to an end and by the 1840's the initiative was passing to the railways which were building up their networks to provide easier and cheaper travel. The first regular train service in Northern Ireland was opened on the Belfast to Lisburn line by 'Ulster Railway Company' in 1842 and their terminus building was at Glengall Street, later to become part of Great Victoria Street Station.

A horse drawn carriage service connected Knock with Belfast from 1870-1899. Also in the 1870's, municipal horse-drawn trams were introduced to many Belfast streets across the Lagan – but only to the inner reaches of East Belfast. Early routes from Castle Junction included Botanic, Ormeau, Windsor Avenue, York Street, Lower Antrim Road, Bridge End and Albertbridge Road as far as Connswater Bridge. Knock was finally reached in about 1899. By 1905 a fully electrified and expanded tramway system reached all the major suburban areas and the neat avenues and parades of fine new 'plump and prosperous villas' in Knock and beyond. This is the story of some of those people, the houses and community they lived in and how it has all changed over the years.

Beaconsfield
56-58 Knock Road

Our story begins at Beaconsfield (later known as Beacon Field and then Beaconfield), a large house that was originally on the site of the Marie Curie Hospice at the corner of Knock Road and Kensington Road.

(Courtesy of Tony Merrick by Fred Arthur Hurley)

Beaconsfield in 1895

The house was constructed in around 1868 and the first resident was Joseph Miller who operated as an insurance agent at 83 Victoria Street, Belfast. The County Down Name Book locates Beaconsfield as....*a villa residence in the district of Knock 16 chains (350 yards) south south-west of Knock Station.*

By 1893 Beaconsfield was owned by Fred Thomas Hurley who was a tea merchant and had a business at 58 Waring Street. Fred Thomas married Rowena Hutchings in 1870 and the family included Charlotte b.1872, Fred Arthur b.1873, William b.1875, Rowena b.1878 and Henry Hutchins b.1881. They worshipped at St Columba's Church of Ireland on the King's Road (then called Church Road) and Fred Thomas Hurley was elected People's Church Warden in 1897. The church had only been consecrated in 1896 and Campbell College had recently opened in 1894. Fred's younger son Henry Hutchins Hurley was in one of the very first intakes of pupils to the new school.

The first recorded Belfast address for the Hurley's was at Cromac Park Terrace, Ormeau Road in 1880 and by 1883 they had moved to Cremorne Villa, Holywood Road, Strandtown. In 1893 they arrived at Beaconsfield and stayed until 1908 when they moved to Chlorine Gardens, Malone.

Tony Merrick is the great-grandson of Fred Thomas Hurley and his grandmother Rowena Hurley married Alexander Merrick, solicitor of University Street, Belfast on 3 April 1907 at a service at St Columba's Church of Ireland on the Kings Road. Tony Merrick tells the story of how Fred Thomas Hurley from Dublin came to live at Beaconsfield on the Knock Road.

Tony Merrick*: My great-grandfather Fred Thomas Hurley came from Dublin in the 1860's to Belfast probably to find work and his first Belfast address was at Winton's Hotel in High Street which was destroyed in a bombing in the 1970's. He met Rowena Hutchins in 1868. Rowena's father was a Church of Ireland clergyman who came late to the church at aged 50 and in 1872 became Rector of Markethill Parish Church in Co Armagh. By a coincidence his son became Rector of a neighbouring parish in the same year. Fred Thomas Hurley and Rowena Hutchins got married in August 1870. Rowena was just 17 years old and it was a perfect love match and they had 52 glorious years together until he passed away in Sept 1922.*

(Courtesy of Tony Merrick)

The Hurley family in 1883 at Cremorne Villa, Holywood Road now the site of the Job Centre. They moved to Beaconsfield in 1893. From left: Fred Thomas, Rowena, Fred Arthur, mother Rowena with baby Henry and William.

They lived at a house called Cremorne Villa on Holywood Road in the 1880's before moving to Beaconsfield in 1893. (Cremorne Villa, a large Victorian semi-detached was at 106 Holywood Road and before demolition in the 1980's was the Vicarage for St Patrick's Church, Ballymacarrett and is now the Job Centre facing Strandtown PSNI station)

They came through a lot together and endured the tragic loss of their 1ˢᵗ born child Charlotte who died in 1875 of scarlet fever. In 1914 their eldest son Fred Arthur was killed in a motor crash near Johannesburg, S.Africa aged 41. He was a very brilliant Chief Civil Engineer working on the construction of the Sifta barrage project, part of the Aswan Dam works in Egypt between 1900 and 1902.

He met an untimely end. The Great War had just started and Fred decided to enlist as a commissioned officer. But he let it be known in South Africa that he was on his way to enlist. As his chauffeur driven car was rounding a bend a slit trench that had been dug in the road (it must have been dug for him as there were just no other cars around) and the open style car turned over. The chauffeur was killed instantly - and the car came down on top of uncle Fred shattering his spine and he died the next day. It was never proved but the feeling in the family was that it must have been German agents. It took 2 months to bring his body back home due to the danger of ships being torpedoed by U-boats on the long journey back to Belfast.

But he was brought home in January 1915 to the Hurley family home in Chlorine Gardens where he lay overnight. There was a very big turnout at his funeral the next day. This was a blow from which his parents never really recovered.

The inscription on the headstone reads:

**Frederick Arthur Hurley F.C.H., A.M. INST.C.E
Assistant Director of Irrigation, Union Of South Africa
who died near Johannesburg 30th November 1914
as a result of a motor car accident, interred here on
2nd January 1915**

(Courtesy of Tony Merrick)

On the left is a 1910 portrait of keen amateur photographer Fred Arthur Hurley aged 37 and on the right his mother Rowena in 1887 aged 34. In 1895 Fred Arthur acquired a half-plate camera and tripod and made a wonderful photographic record of many Knock scenes including Beaconsfield, Knock Station, newly opened Campbell College and the Presbyterian Church and Post Office at the Stye Brae.

(Courtesy of Tony Merrick by Fred Arthur Hurley)

The caption reads: 'August 1895, Campbell College, the Hawthorden Road entrance'. Campbell College was opened on 3rd September 1894 on a 70 acre estate bought by the trustees of Henry James Campbell (owner of Mossley Mills) from Sir Thomas McClure. On the opening day there were 213 boys on the register which included No.91, Henry Hurley (younger brother of the photographer) while John Archer jnr (see 60 Knock Road) was no.14, Henry Clegg, son of the Newmarket Lodge owner (at 32 Knock Road) was No. 36, Robert Garrett of Lanaven, (17 Kensington Road) was No.73 and Samuel Watson (of Rosemount) was No.204. All four new boys may have entered this gateway on their first day at Campbell College.

It is interesting how social norms and expectations have changed over the years. Tony Merrick reminded me that whilst on the one hand the death of F.A.Hurley was a tragedy and his loss from the Hurley family point of view was incalculable, on the other hand during the Victorian/Edwardian period the middle classes loved nothing so much as a 'great funeral'. It was also a great social occasion too and a chance for the obituary writer to reflect on the achievements of a very purposeful and worthy life.

The News Letter carried an obituary on 23rd January 1915 with the heading 'Remains brought from South Africa' and went on to observe that 'the remains of this gentleman were interred yesterday in the City Cemetery, the impressive burial service being conducted by the Very Rev Wm Dowse, Dean of Connor and the Rev F.W. Austin M.A., Rector of St Columba's, Knock.' The article goes on to list the 'chief mourners', who were all men and mentions the deceased's schooling. He had attended Methodist College and then Trinity College, Dublin. When he attended The Royal Indian Engineering College he 'had a most distinguished career, winning many prizes'.

It seems Fred Hurley was able to bring in major engineering projects on time and within budget and 'he received special praise from Lord Cromer and Sir William Garsten and was decorated by the Khedive with the Order of Medjihich. As an indication of the high-esteem in which he was held it may be noted that the High Commissioner for South Africa wrote a letter of sympathy to the Hurley family expressing his government's high appreciation of the irrigation work carried out. A memorial service was held in Pretoria during which public offices were closed and there were many expressions of regret at the loss sustained through the untimely end of such a valuable life.'

Tony Merrick: My great grandfather seemed to think that Fred was destined to receive a knighthood and to that end he had commissioned a professional genealogist to prepare the Hurley Family tree. The genealogist prepared the family tree and it seems he traced it right back to the Middle Ages. My grand mother remembered bits of it and the Hurleys originally came from County Offaly where there was some castle, which belonged to the family in the late middle ages.After Fred Arthur was killed my great grandfather lost heart completely and he deposited the family tree in the Public Records Office at the Four Courts, Dublin which was burned to the ground in 1922 thus taking with it the Church of Ireland parish records, deeds and wills.

The Beaconsfield drawing room and the baby grand piano which was played by Rowena Hurley.

As there was no photocopying then, the one and only copy was lost along with all the source documents and with the result that now anything before 1815 or so is not available whereas if the fire had not happened we would have the whole story going back to the 14th or 15th Century – very sad.

The Hurleys came from quite a distinguished line and they were very aggressive and forth right type of people. My grand mother told me their family motto was **Clear the Way**. (Clear the Way or in Gaelic: 'Faugh a Ballagh' was also the motto of the Royal Irish Fusiliers). If certain members of the family were anything to go by then they lived up to that name. An example was Fred Arthur who one day in 1900 when he was home on leave and he and Rowena (my grand mother) were walking arm-in-arm in Donegall Place (as people did in those days) and an ignorant man was walking along reading a newspaper and not looking where he was going. He knocked into my grand mother and instead of apologising just walked on – without a moments hesitation, Fred Arthur walked after the man and tapped him on the shoulder then punched him on the jaw as hard as he could and knocked him out cold. Then he and Rowena continued their stroll. That's the type of man he was.Later when he was in Egypt he had a fox terrier, which he took with him from Belfast and some Arab children stoned the dog to death. Fred Arthur punished the entire village by putting an unpleasant tasting chemical (not a poison) into the village well to make it undrinkable so that the villagers had to walk 5 miles to the next village in a baking temperature of 120F. You did not mess about with Fred Arthur. He was very much a man of action. As another example of Fred Arthur's tough nature he sacked one of his Arab workers in Egypt and the worker sought a reference. In those days employers had to give a reference so he wrote:

"This man is a liar and a thief – Signed Fred Arthur Hurley."

Fred Arthur was also a keen amateur photographer. He had a lovely half-plate camera mounted on a tripod, which gave very sharp pictures. During 1895 he took pictures of many scenes in the Knock area and these have survived remarkably well until the present day. His father was a tough man too. My grandmother Rowena (named after her mother) could have been a professional concert pianist and I can remember her in her late 70's playing Liszt and Chopin and she was a joy to listen to. She did want to become a professional pianist and at 18 made her wishes known to her parents but they said:

"No, you would only live in poverty and there is no telling what strange artistic people you would meet and what bad influence they will have on you."

Grandmother was absolutely heart-broken. There was even pleading from her mother's father Reverend Hutchins as he was a musical man – but it made no difference. In those days parental authority was not questioned. To the day my grandmother died she bitterly regretted that missed opportunity in her life. She was one of the people who had a great influence on my life. She inspired in me my love of local history and she was a very vital person. I was only 14 when she was struck down by a very bad stroke but I did get to know her well. Her influence is lasting. She was a wonderful person who was immensely kind though formidable and not to be trifled with. She died in 1966 at the age of 88 years and created a great impression on those who met her.

Next door to Beaconsfield in 1908 at 60 Knock Road a new house was under construction. By then the Hurley family children had grown up and left home. Tony Merrick's grandmother Rowena had married solicitor Alexander Merrick the year before at St Columba's church. Beaconsfield was sold to a printer called Joseph McBride. In 1922 the householder is listed as J.G. Hillis, linen business and by 1930 James S Gordon, Permanent Secretary to the Ministry of Agriculture had taken up residence.

Margaret Scarisbrook lived across the road from Beaconsfield and recalls Beaconsfield during this period: *The Gordons lived at Beaconsfield across the Knock Road from our house (Dundela) and I remember the house being old and dilapidated. Apparently there was dry rot in the floorboards. There was obviously no keen gardener in the family as it was not a well-kept place and quite neglected. I was friendly with the girl in the Gordon family as she was about my age.*

John Lewis lived in Shandon Park in the 1940's and he remembers visiting Beaconsfield: *I remember Beaconsfield when I was about 8 years old. It was late afternoon and getting dark. Myself and a friend heard that an elderly lady lived there and we were determined to go and see her. We looked in the window and we saw an old woman who seemed to be living in a dishevelled old house. We did not stay for long as we found what we were looking for and of course we were trespassing.*

(Courtesy of Linenhall Library from Belfast News-Letter)

Beaconsfield in 1960 shortly before demolition

Miss Alice Maud Crawford (apparently one of the 'Crawfords' of Crawfordsburn) was the final Beaconsfield resident. She was born in 1866 and was the only daughter of Annie Alicia (1839-1867) who died at only 28 years of age and William Crawford (1829-1907). Alice had two older brothers, William (1863-1929) and Robert (1865-1939) and a younger brother Arthur (1867-1919). Arthur was born on 4th December 1867 and his mother died only 2 weeks later on 19th December. Alice lived in Beaconsfield from 1935 until her death in 1960 aged 94 and the house lay empty for a while and fell into a state of disrepair.

(Courtesy of Roy McConnell)

The 1960's letterhead of the Marie Curie Hospice, Belfast. Note the name of the Secretary, Bernard Robinson

THE MARIE CURIE MEMORIAL FOUNDATION

Patron : Her Majesty Queen Elizabeth the Queen Mother

Chairman :
Ronald W. Raven, Esq.,
O.B.E., T.D., F.R.C.S.

Vice-Chairman :
The Rt. Hon. The Earl of Wemyss and March,
LL.D., D.L., J.P.

Hon. Treasurer :
Major The Lord Amherst of Hackney, C.B.E.

Secretary :
S/Ldr. T. Bernard Robinson, F.C.C.S.

124 SLOANE STREET, LONDON, S.W.1.

BEACONFIELD NURSING HOME

Matron : MISS U. L. JOHNSTON, S.R.N.
'Phone : Belfast 6 5 3 7 5 1

KENSINGTON ROAD
BELFAST, BT5 6NF

In May 1961 Squadron Leader Bernard Robinson (incorrectly named in local newspapers as Bernard Ferguson), secretary of the Marie Curie Memorial Foundation, London announced their plans to buy Beaconsfield, demolish the house and build a nursing home for cancer patients on the site. Beaconfield Nursing Home was opened at a cost of £120,000 in August 1965. The new extension was completed in September 2006 at a cost of £3.5m.

Owen Varra
60 Knock Road

Left is Owen Varra as it looked in 1908 not long after completion. The Archer family had previously lived for many years in a semi-detached house called 'Home Villas' in Kensington Road before their move to Owen Varra. In the picture are John Archer and his wife Mary. The young lady in the deckchair could be youngest daughter May or one of elder sisters Fannie-Annie, Louisa or Mary who continued to live in the house for many years until the 1970's. On the right is the house as it looked in 2005 – not much need for a croquet pitch these days and it is now a car park.

Owen Varra was next door to Beaconsfield and from its completion in around 1908 the Archers were the only family who lived in the house until it was sold in 1971. John Archer operated a clothing business from 24 Arthur Street, Belfast and has been described in various records as: merchant tailor, draper and clothier. He married Mary McMaster in York Street Presbyterian Church on 21st December 1865 and the Rev Henry Cooke, "The Black Man" whose statue commands the front of Royal Belfast Academical Institution at Wellington Place, Belfast, conducted the ceremony.

The Archers previously lived at a fairly new semi-detached house from the 1860's called Home Villa (now 76-78 Kensington Road) with an address at Knock Avenue Road. With re-naming and re-numbering of roads in later years this address would become 76 Kensington Road.

The family included four girls: Mary, Louisa, Fannie-Annie and May plus two boys: John jnr and William.

John Archer jnr was born on 17th February 1879 and attended Campbell College on its opening day in September 1894 (as did Henry Hutchings Hurley who lived at Beaconsfield). He qualified as a solicitor in 1904 and entered the service of Belfast Corporation initially as legal assistant and then in 1906 as Managing Clerk at a salary of £200 per year. He was appointed Town Clerk in 1935 and during the Blitz in 1941 the name of John Archer often appeared on public notices.

It was also his duty to identify the remains of people killed during the air raids. Saint George's market was used as a mortuary during April and May 1941 when 255 corpses were laid out for identification but many bodies and parts of bodies could not be identified. The Campbellian carried the obituary of John Archer jnr and noted that identification of the air raid victims was: *A distressing task, especially when one encountered a bulky parcel labelled simply "Believed to be a mother and five children"*

John Archer jnr retired in 1941 aged 62 at which time he, his wife and son lived at 32 Knockdene Park. In the Public Records Office there is a copy of a letter from the Lord Mayor, Rt Hon Crawford McCullagh thanking John Archer jnr for his service to the Corporation:

(Courtesy of Deputy Keeper of the Records, Public Record Office of Northern Ireland from LA7/50E/1)

Caption reads: *'Belfast Corporations tribute to Mr John Archer (centre) who has retired from the office of Town Clerk, Belfast by the Lord Mayor and members of the Corporation'.*
It looks like the photographer forgot to say "Smile"

The Belfast Street Directory indicates that John Archer was the householder of Owen Varra until 1930 at which time the listing passed to Miss Mary Archer. Interviews with local residents on the Knock Road (with long memories) reveal that at least one other sister also continued to live in the house and she was Miss Louisa Archer who was an accomplished musician. When the last Miss Archer died in 1971 there was an auction at Owen Varra. Local resident Mrs J.Dibble who lived for many years at 23 Cherryvalley Gardens remembers the occasion very well:

Mrs Dibble: Miss Archer had lived at 60 Knock Road and after she died in about 1971 we saw that they were selling the contents of the house. In the advert they mentioned that there were music books for sale and Brenda (my daughter) and I went to see what they were like as Maureen (my other daughter) played the piano. They had an auctioneer and there was quite a big crowd and I bid for some of the classical music books, which eventually I got. The music books were kept in a lovely cabinet – which I thought I had bought as well – but when I came to collect my purchase it was really funny because the music books were sitting in a pile on the floor and somebody else had bought the cabinet!

What seemed like very good value for money during the bidding now seemed very expensive. The music books have the hand written signature "L. Archer" for Louisa Archer and on some of the books there are embroidered covers and as you can see, they are still in beautiful condition.

The Belfast Street Directory indicates that after the auction John. J. Doyle occupied Owen Varra and in 1999 Marie Curie acquired the house to be used as the headquarters of the fund-raising team. Another local resident Joan Shields (nee Doherty) also has a memory of Miss Archer:

Joan Shields: Yes I remember Miss Archer well. She was small, alert and alive but quite old when I knew her. On one occasion she was in bed ill and the surgery was telephoned for the doctor to come out to the house. Apparently there were two doctors with the surname of Graham. Anyway the Doctor Graham who was not Miss Archer's GP made the house call and Miss Archer who was sitting up in bed in a poorly lit bedroom said: "You are not my Doctor!" Dr Graham reported that Miss Archer was very alert for her age.

Margaret Scarisbrook has childhood recollections of the Archers: *Next door to Beaconsfield was Owen Varra and the entrance gate was immediately opposite our home Dundela, 95 Knock Road. The Archers lived at Owen Varra and their garden by contrast with Beaconsfield was wonderful. They had a great gardener who kept the place in immaculate condition and their house was kept the same. I remember John Archer who was Town Clerk of Belfast but I can't remember the names of his 2 sisters as they were very much older than me. In those days you did not call older people by their Christian names so I addressed the ladies as Miss Archer because that was the polite thing to do and they called me Margaret because I was a child. They were charming people and very popular at Knock Presbyterian Church where I went to Sunday School and the teacher Mrs Watson gave us sweets – which meant that we looked forwards to Sunday mornings.*

Mrs Catriona Murray who lives on the Isle of Skye provided some further insight to the Archer story. Her mother, Florrie McCaw had lived at 116 Kensington Road during the early 1900's. She left Belfast when she got married to live in Scotland although she returned to visit over the years. (See later story on Lalghar School and Grianan)

Catriona Murray: I was born in Glasgow and have never been to Kensington Road to the best of my knowledge. I recall the name of Owen Varra as my mother used to visit Miss Archer on her return visits to Belfast from home in Scotland. Miss Archer was my mother's music teacher. My sister remembers visiting Miss Archer just after the war when travel was permitted again. My mother, Florrie McCaw, records in her diary that I also received a birthday present from Miss Louisa Archer. My mother attended Dundela Sunday School in 1897 and the Archers were members of the church during that period.

Mrs Murray has also helpfully pointed me in the direction of 'Who's Who?' where there is an entry for Sir Ernest Henry Murrant (1889-1974) KCMG, MBE. He was a leading figure in all matters maritime during the 1930 – 1950 period and as well as holding directorships in Barclays Bank and many shipping companies he was a representative for the Ministry of War Transport in the Middle East from 1941 – 1944 and became President of the Council of British Shipping in 1947.

Who's Who reports that: *in 1914 he married May, youngest daughter of John Archer, Belfast.*

(Courtesy of Mrs Catriona Murray)

Dundela Presbyterian Church Sunday School in 1897(the name of Knock Presbyterian Church would be adopted by 1921). In the photo is Florrie McCaw, front row, 7th from left in black outfit with white collar. The caption also notes the presence (somewhere) in the group of the Reverend James Hunter who at this time lived in the manse at 13 Kensington Road. Also in the picture are Mrs Archer, Louisa Archer and May Archer.

Dundela
95 Knock Road

(Courtesy of the Molyneaux family)

A 1920's view of Dundela, 95 Knock Road with George and Margaret Molyneaux standing in the doorway. It was located on the entrance to Knockcastle Park facing the gates of Archer home Owen Varra at 60 Knock Road. George was a keen gardener and the garden was 4.5 acres.

Dundela Villa was located directly across the Knock Road from Owen Varra and the earliest mention in the Belfast Street Directory is for 1901 when the householder was John Pyper, jeweller. The County Down Name Book locates Dundela Villa as: *a villa residence 4 chains (75 yards) south of Rosemount.* Margaret Scarisbrook (nee Molyneaux) and her brother Cecil Molyneaux lived at Dundela Villa (they knew it simply as Dundela) during the 1930's and 1940's.

Margaret Scarisbrook: *We lived at a house named Dundela although the map describes it as Dundela Villa. My mother was Margaret Miller and she married George Molyneaux. They were married in about 1914 and Dundela was their first home. My father had one son and three daughters from a previous marriage but they have all been dead for many years. The eldest son was in the Royal Flying Corps and he was killed at the age of 21 in 1918. He is buried in Belfast City Cemetery.*

In my family I had one sister and one brother. I was born in 1916 and my sister was called Doris and she was 3 years younger than me. I was born in a nursing home. My brother is Cecil Molyneaux and he is 8 years younger. Dundela had about 4.5 acres of garden and my father was a great gardener. He used to grow wonderful roses and daffodils in the front garden. In the side garden he grew all types of vegetables and summer fruit such as strawberries and raspberries. There were also tomatoes in a greenhouse and an orchard which was about a half acre in size and we kept hens too as there was plenty of space for them to run about.

The house itself was very pleasant and had a good-sized entrance hall. To the right there was a drawing room and a morning room. There was a large sitting room to the left plus a kitchen and a maid's room. Upstairs there were 4 bedrooms plus a little box room.

Cecil Molyneaux: *Dundela was quite spacious and also had a basement apartment where a family called Davidson lived. There was quite a slope to the ground at the rear of the house and access was gained through a separate side door. We did not have a back door only a front door.*

Margaret Scarisbrook: *The Knock Road was in the country back then and we had a gas street lamp right on the main road in front of our garden. The lamp man came every night and lit the lamp.*

(Courtesy of the Molyneaux family)

George and Margaret Molyneaux with baby Doris and daughter Margaret in 1920

I went to school at Methodist College and my father used to drive me there. But I had two friends Betty & Marjorie Brown who travelled to school on the train. I thought this was a much more exciting way to travel so I was allowed to go with them. They called at Dundela, and we walked to Knock Station where we got the train which cost ½ penny. We took a tram from the station at Queens Quay to Castle Junction and then switched tram to Methody, which cost another 1 penny. It was quite an adventure.

When my father drove he took the route over the Hillfoot Road, then down a little lane called Lovers Lane (Rosetta Road?) which came out at the top of the Ormeau Road and across to the embankment (Annadale Avenue?) to the Stranmillis Road and then on to Methody. Father then went on to his business, which was called Sloan Molyneaux & Co Ltd. There were factories at Pakenham Street off Donegall Pass and the other in Maxwell Street, Sandy Row. The business remains in family ownership.

I had been living in Switzerland during the 1930's and came home to Belfast in 1939. I had booked to fly back to Switzerland again when I received a letter in September from British Imperial Airways saying that they were terribly sorry that they had to cease flights while the war was on. However as soon as peace was resumed they would let me know and get me on the first available flight home. As we know the war went on for the next 6 years and Imperial Airways disappeared so I never did receive notification about the flight. Of course all my clothes were left at my home in Switzerland and I did not get them back. I eventually went to England where I got married. A few years later my husband and I went to Switzerland, and I found that all my clothes had been given away to war refugees.

Cecil Molyneaux: The three houses beside Dundela were 97, 99 & 101 Knock Road and were built by my father in the 1930's on the site of our vegetable garden and the tennis court. They cost £700 each to build. I remember playing on the building site. Part of the Knock Road had been widened, but it was narrow at this point, although it was better than a country lane – but if you met another car you had to drive carefully past it. In 1959 they had widened the road and took some ground from Dundela and the 3 houses.

George Molyneaux died in 1955 and the family left the house, which was then bought by a builder who subsequently knocked it down. Knockcastle Park now goes right through the site of Dundela.

(Left, Courtesy of the Molyneaux family and right, Courtesy of the Knock Golf Club Limited)

The gardens are again well kept in this late 1930's view of Dundela. A couple of changes from the earlier picture are that a window has been inserted over the front door to create a sunroom for Margaret. Also a house (one of three) has been built next door at 97 Knock Road by George Molyneaux who was also Captain of Knock Golf Club during 1928-1930.

Margaret Scarisbrook: *I remember a beautiful house next door to us, which had great ornate lamps at the front entrance. It was called The Orchard and our neighbours were called Alderman and Mrs Duff. (Mr Duff was James Augustine Duff. In 1925 he was elected Stormont MP for East Belfast. He was also High Sheriff of Belfast in 1923. The Duffs lived at The Orchard from c.1916-1932 then moved to Belmont). In my younger days in the 1920's the Orchard was a beautiful house. Every room was lovely. In the house I saw my very first ensuite bathroom. They also had an unusual spiral shower which when you stood in it showered your whole body from head to toe in little sprays of water. I remember being so impressed that I could not wait to get home and tell my parents to get one of these. My father was not convinced and said that our bathroom was perfectly good enough.*

I believe Mrs Duff had been a nurse in her younger days, which was fortunate because one day she saved me from terrible burns. My grandmother was staying with us one day. When I came in from the garden she said that there was a smell of gas coming from the kitchen. She gave me a lighted taper and told me to open the oven door, which of course I did and as I put the taper into the oven it exploded in my face!

I was very badly burned and went rushing out of the house into the garden. At that moment Mrs Duff was passing by and she took me into her house and covered the burns on my face with a sheet of cotton wool and olive oil. My parents were shocked and I was taken immediately to the doctor for treatment. The doctor said that it was very fortunate that Mrs Duff intervened otherwise I would have been scarred for life. As a result I have always remembered Mrs Duff very fondly.

Behind our house there were houses called Rosemount and Rosevale and I cant remember the names of the families because we did not have much contact. Both houses had lanes, which took the entrances away from Dundela so they did not have to pass our house. To the rear of Dundela there were 2 acres of ground which lay empty, and father let this to Mr Mercer who started a garden nursery. He eventually did so well that he bought a more substantial plot of land at the top of Gilnahirk where he now has a nursery.

Mr Hill Mercer was father of Trevor Mercer who along with other members of the family remains actively involved in the continuing success of Hillmount Nursery Centre to the present day. Trevor has very clear memories of the origins of Hillmount in the 1930's.

Knock Road probably hadn't changed much from the 1930's when this photograph, looking from the junction with Sandown Road, was taken in 1959 just before road widening works began. On the left in the distance are Dundela, 95 Knock Road and 97 – 107 Knock Road

A wider Knock Road in 2007 looking from the junction with Sandown Road. The road on the left is the back entrance to Police HQ at Brooklyn and was originally a lane called Rosevale Park which led to several houses including Rosevale Cottage. There are plans afoot to widen the road yet again after the 1959 attempt was postponed due to objections by Knock Road residents.

The Orchard in 2007 hides behind a high wall on the Knock Road facing the Marie Curie Hospice. The house was built in 1916 and James Duff MP was resident until 1932 when Mrs Mary Finlay of Finlay's Soap and Candle Works became the householder and lived there until 1960. Alexander Finlay had established his soap and candle making business in Belfast in 1798. A huge variety of Finlay's prize-winning soaps were available from the substantial Victoria Square factory until 1955 when the business was closed and the premises sold. The Orchard has been vacant for several years since the Gibson's left and according to the signage of various estate agents, is due for demolition and redevelopment.

(Courtesy of Trevor Mercer, Hillmount Nursery Centre)

Left, a young Trevor Mercer outside the family shop at Lomond Avenue and right, cultivating his first market garden at Dundela, Knock Road. His first customer was Margaret Molyneaux.

Trevor Mercer: *My father Hill Mercer came from a market gardening family in Hillhall near Lisburn. From 1936 to 1939 he rented three green houses from Mrs Watson who owned Rosemount, a large house on the Knock Road. She ran a boarding house for paying guests. I remember the greenhouses very well as they were attached to the main house. There was also a conservatory with a patterned floor and a pond in the middle. A lean-to glasshouse and a traditional glass sided greenhouse, set at right angles to it, were all connected.*

Rosemount's main entrance was opposite Beaconsfield gate lodge and it lay behind Judge Gibson's house (The Orchard). During the 1940's the Finlay family who were soap manufacturers with a factory in Victoria Square, Belfast, owned The Orchard. (The Belfast Street Directory for 1943 records that the resident of The Orchard was indeed Mrs Mary Finlay, Rosemount Nursery).

In addition to the greenhouses at Rosemount my father rented some land from the Molyneaux's next door at Dundela where my father encouraged me to have my first garden. Mrs Molyneaux was also a regular customer of my father. The first flower, I grew, was Cosmos and Mrs Molyneaux was the first customer to buy some from me. The ground at Rosemount and Dundela was very fertile and we grew some vegetables too. There was also an orchard and in the centre was a great big pear tree, which produced lovely sweet pears. We would pick the pears and store them in the attic of our shop at Lomond Avenue (run by my mother Lily) where they were wrapped in paper and placed on trays until they ripened. This was at a time when imported fruit was very scarce and the pears sold well in our shop. It was from here that my father heard about a smallholding for sale on the Upper Braniel Road opposite Stewart's Nursery, which was owned by a son of J.L.Stewart, founder of Stewarts Cash Stores.

My father and mother put many hard hours into the early years of developing the foundations of the business that is here today. Their standards were high and we had to follow suit. One principle my father taught me, along with many others, was never to owe or borrow money. My father and my brother John worked the smallholding at Gilnahirk. The family knew it as 'The Place' until, in 1942, when the first greenhouse was built, a proper business name was required. Hill Mercer was the owner, so that gave the first part of the name and of course the elevation – mount was the appropriate second half – hence the name 'Hillmount'.

Hillmount was bought at auction for a sum of £500 and the purchase included a 5-acre smallholding containing three fields and a mud cottage, which had a bedroom, kitchen and byre for two cows. The tenants of the mud cottage were a family called Green who paid a rent of 5 shillings weekly and the gable-end of their house was propped up with long pieces of timber. On noticing the state of the cottage my father told Mr Green to look for other accommodation as he thought the dwelling was unsafe. The Greens moved out in due course – and took their timber props with them. When my father next went to the cottage he found that the wind had blown out the whole gable-end, which was now lying on the side lawn complete with fireplace! I can remember looking at what I thought, at the time, was a very funny sight.

During Easter 1941 father and my brother John worked on the restoration of the cottage and the byre was converted into a scullery and bedroom. At this moment the Blitz hit Belfast. The Mercers then evacuated from Belfast to Gilnahirk. My mother looked after the shop at Lomond Avenue during the day and took the Major bus to Mann's Corner in the evenings. Mr McClements operated the Major bus. 'Big John' let me drive the bus from Gilnahirk School to Mann's Corner.

The Major bus has reached the end of the Cherryvalley route at Mann's Corner. Lily Mercer journeyed from Lomond Avenue to Mann's Corner and then walked to Hillmount Nursery. The Nissen Hut to the right of the bus was the billet for an anti-aircraft searchlight unit during the 1940's. The Major bus was a familiar sight on the Knock Road, Cherryvalley, Gilnahirk route for many years. It was operated in the 1920's by the Clements family and based at Albertbridge Road.

Rosemount
87 Knock Road

(Courtesy of Joy Hill)

Rosemount was located on the site of Knockcastle Park and backed onto Brooklyn. This 1930 view shows part of the long driveway leading to Knock Road with gateway next door to The Orchard. After life as a family home, the house became a boarding house in later years.

68

Rosemount first appears in the Village Directory in 1880 under Knock Village though its exact age is unclear. Thomas Pullman (a handkerchief manufacturer), who is listed as a resident of 'The Knock' as far back as 1868 is known to have resided in Rosemount in 1880. He was followed in 1890 by John Watson and the County Down Name Book locates the house at: *6 chains (130 yards) south of Brooklyn.* Joy Hill (nee Brownlee) was born in 1928 the last of 5 children and spent her early years at Rosemount, her family home and has a good-humoured recollection of those days.

Joy Hill: My mother was Sarah Patterson and she married William Brownlee during the First World War years. They met at a Sunday School picnic at 14 years of age in a church on the Newtownards Road near Westbourne Street. When they got married the plan was to immigrate to America. My father had relations in Hull where they stopped en route to America. They never actually got any further and headed back to settle in Belfast. There is a family heirloom, which is a bible. It is enscribed as a farewell gift to William Brownlee, though of course they never made it to America but got to keep the bible anyway!

When I was born in 1928 the family lived in a house on the Upper Newtownards Road on the right hand side near Rosepark overlooking what is now the Stormont Estate. We moved from Rosepark to a house at 25 King's Road known as St Columba - which was next door to St Columba's Church but confusingly was not actually attached to the church. People were always calling on church business and we had to explain that we had no connection. Not long afterwards during the early war years the family moved again this time to Rosemount on the Knock Road. I remember Rosemount as being filled with family activity. It was a very happy home and quite a large house with a very elaborate conservatory on the south-facing gable wall a bit like a smaller version of the Palm House at Botanic Gardens in Belfast The house had 4 downstairs reception rooms with a kitchen and 7 bedrooms upstairs. It was a typical Victorian house with a double frontage. There was also a large garden plus a field, which I think was about an acre in size with a lovely old gnarled evergreen tree in front of the house. I remember also an enormous Conference Pear tree, which always seemed to be laden with fruit and a few apple trees too.

Behind the trees our neighbour to the rear was a Mrs Coulter who lived in a house called Rosevale. In front of our house was a lovely more modern house than ours called The Orchard where Mrs Finlay lived.

A 1950's view of Rosemount with miniature palm house now built against the south-facing wall. The house was demolished in 1965 to make way for new houses at Knockcastle Park.

My father was a clothing manufacturer with a factory on Chichester Street near the old Plaza Ballroom. He also had a factory in Clones Co Monaghan. I went to Strandtown school because my friend Joan went there and we used to get the tram each morning.

The war came and my father rented a house in Whitehead. (Belfast Street Directories show that Rosemount was rented by HM Government during the 1940's) I went to Whitehead High School, which was a mixed girls and boys school. I was pleased about this. After a couple of years we moved back to Belfast and I went to Bloomfield Collegiate School to join up with my friend Joan again.

A few years later the family moved house again to the Upper Newtownards Road. We lived in the first house after Knock Road, which was number 445 and the house, was called Ardross (now demolished). Our next-door neighbour was well known, he was J.L.Stewart who founded Stewarts Cash Stores and he lived at 2 Knock Road.

Ardross was right on the main Upper Newtownards Road facing Burmah Castrol House, which I think, was constructed during our time there. Our house had very little land around it, which might have been the idea for the move as my parents were getting on in years. Ardross of course is gone too along with the house next door.

My father died in 1955 and my mother stayed on with some other members of the family.

Another house, which I forgot to mention, was Brooklyn, which was not far away at the back of Rosemount. It was used as an army camp during World War Two and also a POW camp for German prisoners. We had a good view of Brooklyn because our driveway at Rosemount went right alongside the recreational area where the Germans played.

I remember one day I was out walking and squinting over at these very handsome young men who were doing their exercises whilst pretending that I was not looking (of course I was a teenager back in those days). It was one of those well-known secrets in the area that these men were German POW's. I can't quite remember how long they stayed at Brooklyn although I suppose it was not that long after the war had ended.

(Courtesy of Police Museum, Brooklyn)

This 1970 aerial view of Knock Road crossing from left to right helps pinpoint names and places. Top centre is RUC HQ at Brooklyn with Rosevale Cottage the white house to the left. The road left is Knockcastle Park which was opened in 1969 through the site of Dundela. The three detached houses bottom left are at 97, 99 and 101 Knock Road. The new houses in the centre of the picture are built on the site of Rosemount with The Orchard in front. Kensington Road is just visible bottom right and Knockvale Park, top left.

(Courtesy of Linenhall Library from Belfast News-Letter)

A burst water main on Monday 23rd November 1959 had caused some subsidence at the junction of Knock Road and Upper Newtownards Road. In the photograph on the left in the top right-hand corner is the Brownlee home at 445 Upper Newtownards Road and alongside is 447 (both demolished). Next door the semi at 449 - 451 with high gable remains in 2007. In the photo on the right the newly built Burmah-Castrol House (now Barnardo's) is in the background. Apparently the driver of the Hillman car, Mr John Roddy was on his way to play golf at Shandon Park Golf Club and was uninjured by the ordeal. He walked the remainder of the journey.

Brooklyn

(Courtesy of Police Museum, Brooklyn)

On the left is a snowy 1930's view of Brooklyn and on the right is a 1960's view which shows that all the chimneys have been removed. Brooklyn was built around the same time as Beaconsfield in 1868 and became RUC police headquarters in 1962. An extensive modern office block has been built onto the south gable-end of the old building. Brooklyn has never had a street number in its address.

Brooklyn is one of only 35 entries in the Village Directory in 1870 for Knock Village when the resident was Alexander O'Rorke and the County Down Name Book locates it as: *a villa residence situated in the district of Knock, 9 chains (200 yards) south west of Knock Railway Station.* The Police Museum is based at PSNI Headquarters, Brooklyn and curator Hugh Forrester maintains a comprehensive history file on the house and the families who lived there.

The first record of Brooklyn is from 6th July 1869 when the original lease was assigned to Alexander O'Rorke, solicitor in the townland of Ballycloughan. By 1874 Brooklyn was occupied by Cumberland-born William Hinde and his name first appears in the Belfast Street Directory in 1863 as a coal merchant based at Queens Quay. He probably chose this location as a business base because it was next door to the Belfast and County Down Railway terminus, which allowed him to transport imported Welsh, Scottish and Cumbrian coal to all parts of the country. The old railway timetables also show that if William Hinde took the 6.18pm train from Queens Quay after a busy day at the office, he would arrive at Knock Station (a 2 minute walk from Brooklyn) at 6.28pm!

Knock had another appeal as William Hinde was a devout Methodist and Knock Methodist Church is only a short walk from Brooklyn. He took an active part in the formation of the church, which had opened in 1870 and was an initial trustee along with future son-in-law Lancelot Shaw and neighbours Edward Emerson who lived across the Knock Road in a grand house called Enderly and Thomas Pullman of Rosemount.

Coal was big business in the nineteenth century and William Hinde built up a fleet of small sailing ships called brigantines, which could easily gain access to shallow harbour ports. By 1880 he owned a fleet of five sailing ships. He was also moving with the times and had bought his first steam ship in 1874. He was elected to Belfast City Council in 1889 for the Cromac Ward although ill health forced him to resign after only a year in office. His doctor advised William Hinde to visit Smedleys Hydrotherapy Establishment in Derbyshire for treatment. While there he was diagnosed as suffering from cancer. He died at Brooklyn on 6th March 1890. The funeral service was held at Knock Methodist Church and the ships in the Port of Belfast had their flags at half-mast. After his death his only daughter Maria Elizabeth Hinde became the sole beneficiary of his £41,000 estate (his wife Maria having died in 1887) which included ownership of his various business interests.

Wedding party of Maria Elizabeth Hinde and Lancelot Shaw at Brooklyn on 28th March 1877

Maria had married Lancelot Shaw in 1877. The circumstances of the marriage were that Maria had been forbidden by her father to marry the man of her choice and she then subsequently married Lancelot who was 20 years her senior – but very much approved of by her parents. They would have a family of seven children. Lancelot became business manager and may have worked for the company prior to his marriage to the boss's daughter.

The business did not fare well and by 1910 it had been sold off. Previously all the coal ships in the William Hinde fleet had been wrecked or sunk and some company offices in Cumbria had been destroyed in a fire. The M3 flyovers and Odyssey complex now occupy the site of the coal business.

The Hinde family moved to Australia where they set up home at a 200,000 acre sheep station in the outback. They never returned to Belfast. Lancelot died in Australia in 1913 while Maria lived on until 1939. Maria had sold Brooklyn in 1905 to John Morton. His name is quite well known in certain Belfast circles as he ran a bottling plant in Ormeau Avenue, which distributed the famous Mortons Red Hand Guinness.

Right, (Courtesy of Keith Thompson) a fine picture of Brooklyn resident William Hinde, 1823-1890, in later years.

Various members of the extended family of Morton, McClure and Melville (well known as funeral undertakers) would live in and own Brooklyn from 1905 until 1949. John Davidson then bought the house and retained ownership until 1953. His daughter Ethel Pierce struck up a correspondence with Mr Wilson of RUC Headquarters in 1981 and provided some background to the occupants:

Ethel Pierce: *Mr Morton McClure whose wife was a Melville bought the house in 1924 and lived there until 1938. It seems various nephews and cousins had the house at various times. The Mortons were bottlers (of beer I imagine). In 1939 the house was let to the army and when my father John Davidson bought the house in 1945 it was in a deplorable mess, gardens and house. He paid £4,500!*

Eventually six gardeners were employed, a greenhouse was built and within a year or two there was a magnificent rose and flower garden with a 500 ft long fence of sweet pea. The gardeners also found a huge white statue at the bottom of the garden, which had a white hand pointing up into the air.

In the house just inside the front door to the right was a large cloakroom, containing a huge safe, which we were unable to open – we had many thoughts of the gold or jewels, which it may contain! It was my job to refurbish the house and detail the ten – yes ten – servants to help my father entertain his many business friends.

Ethel Pierce mentioned that the army had taken up residence in 1939 and Knock resident Roy McConnell, whose family lived at 77 King's Road, has a clear memory of this period.

Roy McConnell: *I remember on Sundays there would be troop trains arriving at Knock Station and they would unload regiments of soldiers at Brooklyn army camp, which is now PSNI headquarters.*

The Middlesex and Gloucester regiments were both at Brooklyn and they subsequently shipped out to join the 8th Army in North Africa. Then the Americans arrived and they spent some time preparing for D-Day. Then all of a sudden they disappeared overnight and the camp lay idle for a while. The next arrivals at Brooklyn were German POW's and apparently they were mostly U-Boat crews who had landed at Londonderry.

(Courtesy of Roy McConnell)

A German U-boat surrenders at Lisahally on the banks of the River Foyle not far from the city of Londonderry. Clusters of similar vessels ended the war here to be later towed out to sea and sunk. This crew could well have spent time at Brooklyn. Lisahally was also the base for the 'mothball' fleet of Royal Navy vessels during the 1950's including the frigate 'Amethyst' of 'Yangste Incident' fame.

I remember walking round to visit some friends in Knockvale Park on the Knock Road not far from Beaconsfield and watched the Germans playing a football match. They lived in Nissen huts, spread out around the field in front of Brooklyn. I never saw them outside the camp. I do remember the military police, the Redcaps, keeping an eye on them. They were eventually transferred to a POW camp in England and that was the end of the war for Brooklyn. It is strange to think of wide-open fields on the Knock Road, which is now a very busy thoroughfare built up with houses.

Jim Allen lived not far from Knock Station at Fountain Villas, 109 Kings Road and tells a story about Brooklyn when it was an army camp back in the 1940's: *I worked in Harland & Wolff. A workmate called Bobby Moffett and a few of his mates, who lived at Ballymacarrett, all joined the army after the outbreak of war. They received instructions to meet at the Belfast & County Down Railway station at Queens Quay at 6.00pm on a certain date. With some excitement and expectation they thought the train would take them to Donaghadee where they would get a boat over to Scotland and see a bit of the world and a bit of the action. After a short train journey (a bit longer if the level crossing gate was closed at Neill's Hill) they arrived at their destination for basic training at an army camp at Brooklyn, Knock Road, East Belfast! As most of them had never heard of Knock they might have been in another country. Anyway they stayed and were confined to camp for the first week and then given some home leave. The funny part of the story was that, when they took the train from Knock to Belfast, they were spotted by friends and neighbours at the Holywood Arches. People immediately assumed that they had gone AWOL from some distant base and made their way back to Belfast.*

Billy MCormick was a firewatcher and member of the Home Guard and he lived at 19 King's Road: *I remember seeing the German POW's from Brooklyn one day. There were about one hundred of them being marched along the Sandown Road and what particularly impressed me was that there were only about two British soldiers on guard duty. I am not sure what they were all doing on Sandown Road but it was possibly to get to the railway station at Neill's Hill. I also remember that there were a lot of khaki tents in the front garden of Brooklyn which the Germans lived in.*

On other occasions I recall seeing troop trains with both British and American soldiers on board and I think they were headed for Ballykinlar Army Camp in County Down.

(Courtesy of Police Museum, Brooklyn)

By 1953 Brooklyn was assigned to the N.I. Ministry of Home Affairs and used for Civil Defence Training. In 1958 the old Brooklyn gate lodge, air-raid shelters and the stable block were demolished. In 1960 builders were contracted for the construction of a new police headquarters building at an estimated cost of £164,500. During the course of the building programme the roof caught fire and delayed the completion by several months and the final cost was actually £180,000. On 24th September 1962 the Inspector General of the RUC and 200 members of staff occupied the new RUC headquarters building. A major extension was completed in 1980.

(Courtesy of Police Museum, Brooklyn)

This 1980 aerial view of Brooklyn shows how the old house has been extended with office buildings over the years. The original 'T'-shaped extension was completed in 1962 and in 1980 further buildings are under construction on the site of Rosevale Cottage. Notice that Knockcastle Park is now fully built up. Top left is Beaconfield Nursing Home (Marie Curie Hospice) and the BCDR railway track-bed is at the foot of the picture and follows the tree-line.

Widening of Hillfoot Road and Knock Road

I risked life and limb, in the name of posterity, by standing in the middle of a busy Knock Road, close to Ascot Park in summer 2007 to take this photograph. The road widening scheme is due (allegedly) to transform this stretch of road into a dual carriageway.

At the time of writing, as a resident of Kensington Gardens I recently joined R.A.C.K.S., which is the Residents' Association of Cherryvalley, Kensington and Shandon. (See the very professional website: www.racks.org.uk.)

I duly received the news sheet and an article caught my eye: *Residents are concerned at the volume and speed of traffic using the area as a 'rat-run'. The proposed widening of the Knock Road and revised junctions with it will seriously exacerbate the problem.*

It turns out that Regional Development Minister, Conor Murphy, has announced major improvements on the A55 Knock Road and £9.7m will be spent on a road-widening scheme between Knockwood Park and the King's Road.

The Minister said: *I am well aware of the need to remove this bottleneck on the Outer Ring Road around East Belfast which carries 38,000 vehicles per day. The impact on the local community and the environment has been a key consideration in deciding the most appropriate solution and I am satisfied that the proposed scheme strikes the best balance between the benefits to the wider public and the effects of road widening through this predominantly residential area.*

The modern Upper Knockbreda Road is now a major arterial route and dual carriageway which carries road traffic from Newtownbreda, along the Outer Ring Road past Cregagh and Castlereagh to Knockwood Park on Knock Road, close to Braniel, where the road narrows into a single carriageway until the Upper Newtownards Road is reached. The dual carriageway then continues from Hawthornden Way to the Tillysburn Junction.

The road was developed in several stages over the years since the 1950's and has altered the character of the whole Knockbreda area which leads to Knock.

Several local historians have described the rural nature of the locality before road widening became a necessity.

(Courtesy of Mike Maybin by RC Jackson)

Looking along the Saintfield Road towards Belfast from the junction with the Hillfoot Road (pre-Supermac) in 1950 as a trolleybus approaches the terminus. Not much traffic then. This photograph illustrates the rural nature of the suburbs with plenty of woodland and hedgerow. By 2007 most of the vegetation has gone and Sainsbury's large store at Forestside now dominates the view on the right. The house far left, near Church Road and facing Galwally, remains today.

(Courtesy of Gavin Bamford from an old postcard)

Taken in 1964, this photo of the new road layout at the junction of the Hillfoot Road and Saintfield Road picks out some old landmarks. Left, Supermac shopping complex and centre the big old house in the grounds of the Drumkeen Hotel. Supermac was demolished in 1996 and Forestside Shopping Centre now stands on the site. The low building right, at the entrance to Upper Galwally, is the Rates Office.

(Courtesy of Ella Ferguson)

A super picture taken on the occasion of the 'Supermac' opening day in 1964. Mrs Green (in fashionable hat and gloves) was the wife of Supermac manager Brian Green and she is being served by Ella Dornan and Peggy Bradley. The till indicates a bill of £8-5s-5d

The contrast between this area today and a century ago was described by Jesse C.Barbour in 'The Rock in the Plain'. He provided a description of Cregagh, only a short journey from Knock, as it was in times past: *The year 1900 seems a long time ago. For most of us, however, 1900 seems more distant still when we are told Cregagh was little more than a rural district. The main road was narrow and rough and it was bounded for the most part by scraggy hedges. Green fields in which sheep and cattle browsed in rural quiet and tranquillity, extended right along to the Castlereagh Road. From Cregagh Presbyterian Church there was rich pastureland right up to the Knockbreda Road and on the opposite side of the road two or three villas had recently been erected. A tramway service, worked by horses, ran right up to the top of the Cregagh Road. In 1905 a regular village sprang up beside Cregagh Glen which was to become one of the most popular suburbs of the city.*

David Hammond described the history of the Church of Ireland at Cregagh in 'St. Finnian's Cregagh, 1932-1982': *As late as 1928 the area was still partly inhabited by dairy farmers who sold milk daily off spring carts in the streets of Belfast* (Ballymaconaghy Dairy, Cregagh was located close to the point where modern Rosetta Road meets the Upper Knockbreda Road). *But as the city continued to develop from the boom years of linen and ship building in the nineteenth century and the new tramway service made travel cheaper and easy, people had spilled out to houses built on each side of the Cregagh Road. Cregagh had acquired a residential character with new developments for ex-servicemen and also at Everton Drive and Downshire* Road (which are first mentioned in the 1907 Belfast Street Directory) *so that green fields were gradually covered with streets of houses and farmers retreated further into the countryside.*

Cregagh had always been part of the Parish of Knockbreda (the church is at Church Road, Newtownbreda) *which had served the old population of farmers and farm labourers for generations. The new population found Knockbreda too remote and in those days the end of the tramlines seemed like the end of the world. Few wanted to traverse the Hillfoot Road (to get to church), then more like a country lane, in all sorts of weather. This new settlement had little sense of neighbourhood and there were few of the patterns of kinship that exist in an older community. There was no school, no social centre, no library and scarcely a community organisation.*

The whole area lay outside the boundary of Belfast, set on a slope looking towards the gantries of the shipyard and the backdrop of Napoleon's Nose at Cavehill and it was surrounded by green field and leafy streams.

(Courtesy of Mike Maybin from R.C.Jackson)

This 1950 view of the Cregagh trolleybus terminus shows that this section of Cregagh Road retained the qualities of a country lane. To the left of the picture is 372 Cregagh Road, now a GP surgery and previously the home of Great War hero, William McFadzean VC. The 1923 Street Directory records that the resident was his father William McFadzean, yarn salesman.

Not much change in the Cregagh village area since 1950 although the road has been widened and the trolley bus overhead cables and garden hedges have gone. The trolley bus turning circle, left and all the houses in the 1950 view have remained into 2007. The tramlines originally extended to the top of the hill where the Cregagh Road met the Hillfoot Road.

Looking in the opposite direction: On 30th December 1954 the News-Letter reported on 'the widening of the junction of Cregagh Road and Hillfoot Road'. This was several years before the construction of the Upper Knockbreda dual carriageway really got underway. Notice how much front garden has been lost in the road widening.

This little scene is barely recognisable in 2007 due to major roadworks and the construction of retaining walls. It is Saturday 10th September 1932 and the clergy are gathered for the consecration of St Finnian's Cregagh. The lane in the background with the parked cars is Knockbreda or Hillfoot Road. The detached house to the far left was known as Cregagh House and was for a time St Finnian's Rectory; it remains today as the Ulster Spine Centre although it is now painted white. To the far right is a red brick semi-detached terrace known as Mountview, now 172 Upper Knockbreda Road. The house centre is probably 2-4 Rocky Road.

(Courtesy of Linenhall Library from Belfast News-Letter)

Further along the Hillfoot Road from St Finnian's looking towards Castlereagh, this great picture which shows how narrow the original Hillfoot Road, right, was in 1959 prior to the road widening scheme which is now fully underway on the left alongside Rochester Road. The roof of Glenburn Methodist Church (built in 1955) is clearly visible above the row of new houses.

Taken from a similar angle in the 1980's, this view of the Hillfoot Road shows how the road system, to the left in this view, has been widened over the years.

A rather grainy view of the junction at Castlereagh Road and Upper Knockbreda Road in 1959 as the new dual carriageway is under construction. In the block of shops, which are now occupied by China Express, Winemark and Domino's Pizza were Hillfoot Service Station and Derek Marsden, confectioner and grocer – well known as a local entertainer.

Marion G.Kelly wrote an article entitled 'From the Troughloney to Upper Knockbreda Road' for the East Belfast Historical Society in 1996. I have been unable to find the name 'Troughloney' in any formal archive such as Ordnance Survey or Street Directory although it apparently ran from Cregagh Road to Rosetta. Likewise the Hillfoot Road which seems to cover that stretch of thoroughfare which we know today as the Upper Knockbreda Road leading from Forrestside Shopping Centre to Castlereagh.

Marion Kelly: From the time we moved to the Hillfoot Road the older residents would invariably want to explain just how important the Troughloney had been in their young lives. It was the favourite walk for romantics, especially on Sunday evenings after church. It seems the youths attended church if only to be in the right place to join their fellow 'danderers' for the ritual procession of girls and boys.

To many there was the distinct advantage in the public lighting, but, of course, the vehicular traffic was much slower and lighter allowing couples time to step aside into the hedges. There were other helpful features of the narrow winding road from the Forster Green Hospital at the junction of the Saintfield Road to the Castlereagh Road and on to Knock and Stormont. This was the direct route for important visitors from Hillsborough Castle so that children could safely wait for Royal parties whose cars had to slow down to negotiate the bends, particularly at the Cregagh Glen and the wee shop. Outside Graham's wee Glen shop and at its wall everyone gathered to see and to be seen. Sadly it was often broken into.

Further along the Hillfoot (it was usual to drop the unnecessary Road) young Billy Graham on Hayes' land made himself a wooden structure for selling newspapers. This was wrecked in a big storm about 1933 providing a real windfall of firewood for the local lads. At the river under Bell's Bridge on the Cregagh Road there was an entrance to the filter beds at Grand Parade on land later developed as Montgomery Road. Before 1948 the only buildings between the new Rochester Avenue and the Castlereagh Road were a row of labourers cottages leaving a clear view of Stormont Buildings.

During the summer of 1959 the local press carried a very modern sounding headline banner and article which proclaimed:

'Knock Residents protest against road widening plan'

Belfast Corporation Improvement Committee is to inspect on July 9 (1959) the section of the Knock Road which will be affected by the proposal to build an 80 foot wide dual carriageway between the city boundary at Clara Park and the old Knock railway station.

This was decided at a meeting of the Committee yesterday when a deputation of residents protested strongly against the proposal. Handing in a petition signed by 100 residents in the area the deputation stated that the scheme would virtually destroy the amenities of the district. Many gardens would be reduced by up to 50 feet and rendering the houses almost unsuitable for family life in an area where there were no open spaces or public parks, nowhere but private gardens where children might play in reasonable safety. The deputation said that while there was no doubt that certain parts of Knock Road needed widened, a dual carriageway was neither necessary nor desirable. Under the scheme Knock Road will be widened to 80 feet to link with an improved highway from Saintfield Road. The plan is designed to facilitate the flow of traffic from Saintfield and Lisburn directions to the Upper Newtownards Road.

The residents statement declared that:' While no system of payment can fully compensate an owner for the loss of large parts of a garden it is most unlikely that the scale of the compensation paid will even cover the financial loss to householders through depreciation in the marketable value of the property. We believe that even if the present speed limit of 30 mph is retained some degree of speeding is inevitable on such a road, bringing with it all the attendant dangers to life and limb in the Knock District.'

The residents claimed that there was no concentration of population or industry beyond the city boundary large enough to require such a roadway. Traffic to and from Newtownards and Comber requiring to by-pass Belfast was small. A large part of the traffic to Bangor originated in Belfast and only a limited part of this traffic could benefit from the proposed road. The other part would be served by the Sydenham by-pass.

A few weeks passed for deliberations and the local press headlined the Belfast Corporation Improvement Committee decision and then seemed to lose interest in the story.

'Second thoughts on Knock Road widening scheme, Committee to recommend new plan'

Belfast Corporation Improvement Committee decided yesterday to recommend that the scheme for building an 80 feet wide dual carriageway along the Knock Road between Clara Park and the old Knock railway station should be abandoned. The committee suggested that a plan should be substituted to bring the road, which is only 30 feet wide in places, up to a uniform width of 50 feet. If widening to 50 feet is approved some residents will lose parts of their gardens but the amount of land to be taken over will be small.

(Courtesy of Linenhall Library from Belfast News-letter)

Belfast Corporation Improvement Committee at Knock Road on 9th July 1959 in front of Ascot Park. The houses in the background are 88, 90 and 92 Knock Road and all have been demolished. Future members of the residents association look on (extreme right) with interest!

(Courtesy of East Belfast Historical Society)

The Hillfoot Road near Braniel as it looked in the 1950's and remembered as 'a narrow and dangerous road' to walk along. A sign (of things to come) beside the bridge says 'Danger – Roadworks Ahead'. The bridge marks the route of a stream which flows through Shandon Park golf course and under the Hillfoot Road on its way to Orangefield.

(Courtesy of Linenhall Library from Belfast News Letter)

A **1959** view shows the beginning of road widening on this part of the **Hillfoot Road**, taken from a point close to **Knockwood Park** and looking towards the **Braniel Estate**. To the left, part of the links of **Shandon Park Golf Club** was lost during the construction of the new dual carriageway. To the right and in the distance through the trees is **Laburnum Cottage**, which would survive until **1969** when **Shandon Park Service Station** was opened on the site. Look closely, the old bridge wall is still there and the remains of the 'Danger-Roadworks Ahead' sign is barely visible just in front of the car.

In 2007 it is hard to imagine the undulations on the old Hillfoot Road before this stretch of the Knock Dual Carriageway was levelled and widened. In the 1800's Knock National School was one of very few buildings close to the site of the present day car showroom on the right of this photograph. On the far left the row of bollards leading to the garage forecourt marks the route of the stream and the old bridge.

Looking along the Knock Road from the Sandown Road junction. The News Letter reported on 21st September 1955 that 'Road widening operations are now in progress at the corner of Knock Road at the junction with Sandown Road'. The houses left are No.133 at the corner and the gable-end of No.131 Knock Road next door.

(Courtesy of Linenhall Library from Belfast News-Letter)

Knock Road in 1959, looking from Cherryvalley in the direction of the BCDR Knock station. The white building on the right, 34 Knock Road, was originally owned by Robert H. Clegg and known as Newmarket stables although by 1948 it was occupied by W.A. Scott & Co, Builders and Thomas Winter, decorator. The forecourt of Miss Lynn's shop at 38 Knock Road is clearly visible on the right beside the parked car which is an Austin Cambridge.

The same Knock Road view in 2007 looking from Cherryvalley to the old railway line which crosses the road at the traffic lights. The roof of Knock Presbyterian Church peeps out on the tree-line.

Spokane and Palermo
42 - 44 & 46 - 48 Knock Road

(Courtesy of Police Museum, Brooklyn)

In 1970 notice the block of semi-detached villas with frontage to Knock Road at the foot of the picture. From bottom right to left: Spokane, Palermo, Casiana and Passadena.

Spokane and Palermo were a development of large, High Victorian semi-detached houses located between Kensington Road and Cherryvalley, facing Brooklyn. The earliest mention of Spokane Villas at 42 and 44 Knock Road occurs in the Village Directory of 1895. The first recorded residents of Spokane were A.F. Porter and James Hicks. At this time 46 and 48 Knock Road was called Hassendean and was the home of James M. Calder. By 1901 it would be renamed Palermo. Knock would not be included under the Belfast Street Directory until 1898.

(In tracing the journey of house names in the Knock area it seems to have been the practice that as new owners moved into the house the name was often changed. Later house names became less fashionable and were dropped altogether as house numbers became the norm in the 1930's).

Stuart Twist lived at 5 Cherryvalley Gardens during the Second World War and as a young man was an enthusiastic member of Cherryvalley ARP No. 457 (more about the defence of the realm and Cherryvalley ARP later in our story), he remembers the role of Spokane in the war effort: *We lived at 5 Cherryvalley Gardens, which was next door to the ARP station at number 3 and they were semi-detached houses. When war broke out in 1939 I remember there were 3 ARP stations in the immediate area. ARP Post 457 was originally in a shop on Gilnahirk Road (now Cherryvalley Bakery beside the butcher J.Williamson & Sons – more later in our story) and then it moved to 3 Cherryvalley Gardens on 4th December 1940. ARP Post 453 was located at a big house called Spokane on the corner of the Knock Road and Cherryvalley although for some reason they called it Cherryvalley Road.*

Then ARP Post 450 was at Neill's Hill with an address at 98 Sandown Road. Spokane was mainly used as a first aid post, and later on, it was used as a canteen for the American troops who were based across the road at Brooklyn from about October 1942. It was a big semi-detached house, and there was a garage near-by. The layout inside Spokane was that the ARP Post was on the 1st floor and the ground floor was for first aid. Dr Fulton conducted lectures and Mr Kelly was in charge of the post. Mr Boyce was the St Johns Ambulance instructor, and he prepared the staff for their first aid exams. My mother was in the first aid team, and, as I was only 16 years old my job was as a messenger for the ARP. I was also used as a casualty in most of their practices - where I was half killed during the procedure!

(Courtesy of Dermot Gallaugher)

Centre and right are early 1980's views of Spokane before demolition due to road-widening plans. In later years these grand old houses were converted into apartments as can be seen from the fire escapes. On the left is a 2007 view of the Spokane corner at Cherryvalley and Knock Road. The field includes the sites of Spokane, Palermo and 1– 2 Passadena which all had entrances directly onto Knock Road. 3 – 4 Passadena, which had an entrance gate onto Kensington Road, survived until 1998 when the Kensington Crescent apartment block was built on the site.

After Spokane had out-lived its usefulness as an ARP Post it reverted to its former role as a family home. Dermot Gallaugher recalls his childhood at Spokane:

Dermot Gallaugher: *My parents were living near London when they married in June 1940 and in 1943 they moved back to Belfast and bought Spokane. The house was large, damp and very draughty and I would never recommend such a house to anybody as a home. It was never in good decorative order.*

Spokane was an old 3 story semi-detached villa. The top floor was an attic in which my father kept a lathe. I had 3 sisters and 2 brothers. The house had a series of landings and staircases, which were great fun to play on. It was probably the idea of my sister Sandra – lets assume she was the leader. Anyway we carried an old tin bath up to the top landing in the attic and filled it with water from jugs. The exciting bit was that we tipped up the bath and the water spilled down onto each floor. The noise prompted Uncle Jim, who was looking after us while our parents had gone out, to emerge from the drawing room to find water flowing everywhere. He spent the reminder of the evening trying to move all the water from around the staircase with a mop into a bucket. I don't think Uncle Jim ever offered to baby sit for us again!

My mother was called Honor Haig and she trained as a nurse. By a coincidence she was brought up about 50 yards from where we lived (Spokane, 42 Knock Road) in a large semi-detached house at 52 Knock Road originally with an address at 2 Passadena. Her family lived there for a few years from 1905 (when the 2 blocks of large semi-detached houses known as Passadena were built) and then during the First World War years moved to a house called Mertoun on Hawthornden Road near Campbell College. The house is long gone but the area is now known as Campbell Chase close to Hawthornden Way. My mother would have been a distant cousin of Earl Haig. There is also a connection with Haig Whiskey although I can't claim any financial benefit arising from that relationship. The Haigs moved to Mertoun and lived there until the late 1930's before moving to Bangor.

My grandfather J.M. Haig was a linen merchant who used to travel home from business in Belfast on the Belmont Road tram and then walk to the house. In 1912 at the time of the signing of the Ulster Covenant, those opposed to the idea were very keen to get the list of names of the signatories.

Two 1920 views of Mertoun, home of J. M. Haig, grandfather of Dermot Gallaugher. The house was located on Hawthorden Road not far from Lord Pirrie's home, Ormiston. A development of modern houses called Campbell Chase at Hawthorden Way now occupies the site.

(Courtesy of Frances Gibson by Alan Seaton)

Looking along Knock Road in 1980 from a position facing the entrance to Knockcastle Park with the wall of the Marie Curie Centre on the right, the tall houses in the centre are Spokane and Palermo (now demolished).

Right, the Marie Curie Hospice in the summer of 2007. The tall board on the tree, right, is the counter for the Living Rooms Appeal which indicates that good progress has been made with the fundraising drive.

For some reason they followed my grandfather from the tram assuming he was a civil servant carrying all the details to the home of Lord Pirrie who lived close by at a large house called Ormiston. They pestered him until he walked directly to the front door of Mertoun and only abandoned their target as he calmly reached into his pocket and produced a door key, which was used to gain admittance!

My father's name was Robert Archer Gallaugher. He was known as Pat because he was born on St Patrick's Day. In the 1930's he was a car salesman with Leslie Porter & Co who were the Riley Agents for Northern Ireland and their showroom was in Great Victoria Street.

My father bought a Riley Lynx car, registration AKB 759 from Artie Bell who was a rider for the Norton Motorcycle Team, and he took part in trial competitions at Craigantlet. He was very keen on motor sports including the Circuit of Ireland, and had a reasonable level of success in the sport. He remained an enthusiastic driver throughout his life. After the war dad started his own car sales business using part of Jack Chambers garage in Donegall Pass.

His next business venture was to buy a catering company called William S. Campbell & Co, which he ran from home. We were often woken by the noise of dishes at all hours of the night, when he came home with Jim Dunn and Mrs McCleery from an outside catering function. As the whole family would not fit into a car we often used the company van for transport. The van had a hatch in the side and we used it to go on holiday like a camper van.

A special event occurred in 1954 when Queen Elizabeth 2 visited Stormont following her Coronation the previous year. There was terrific excitement in Spokane because the royal entourage was to travel in cars from Hillsborough, along the Knock Road and past our house to Stormont. The Knock Road was very narrow in those days, and the footpath had to be negotiated carefully due to the closeness of the passing motor vehicles. It was about half the width of the present road, but it had a huge amount of traffic even then.

Over the years they straightened the route, widened it and removed a lot of dips so that there was a fairly level driving surface. I remember seeing horses and carts laden with hay as they came in from the country.

The Gallaugher family at Portrush in 1952. From right, parents Pat and Honor with Patricia, Sandra, Dermot, Jane, Alastair and Colin. All six Gallaugher children were born between 1941 and 1948.

(Courtesy of Dermot Gallaugher)

Pat Gallaugher 'revving- up' at the Craigantlet Hill-Climb in the 1930's. Notice the RAC marshall to the right in full military type regalia with officer style peaked cap. No crash helmets for racing drivers back then!

114

Anyway Mum hung out her Scottish flag and many of our relatives (mostly old aunts) were invited for tea and sandwiches to witness the procession and eventually "She" was driven past in quite a sedate manner. Mum always claimed that "She" waved to Spokane having noticed the Scottish flag.

Just across Cherryvalley from Spokane was a well-known business on the Knock Road and it was locally known as Miss Lynn's. Originally Miss Lynn had a wee, green, timber shop and it was open 6 days a week and sold everything including newspapers. She had a fox terrier called Roger which was a very effective guard dog. Miss Lynn's was like a community centre for local knowledge (gossip) in the Knock area. She lived around the corner, and walked home to Kilhorne Gardens stopping to talk to everybody she met.

The Belfast Street Directory records that Newmarket Cottage was situated between Knock Railway Station and Cherryvalley and first occupied by Miss E.B. Lynn, Confectioner and J. McBurney, Decorator in 1932. Her next-door neighbour beside the railway station was Robert Clegg who from 1898 is listed at Newmarket Lodge as a horse dealer and operated a posting establishment, stables and garage so that people could travel by horse to the station and then leave their steed in safe hands whilst they travelled off by BCDR train.

Local historian H. Crawford Miller remembers Harry 'Geezer' Clegg operating from a white building where he had stables and horses plus a riding school. The land was soft and boggy beside the Knock River and he recalls a horse getting into difficulty. They used ropes and another horse to pull it out of the mud.

John Keenan recalls the stables close to Knock Station:

John Keenan: *In the 1930's my parents used to go riding there although by the 1940's it had closed. It was located just on the other side of the fence beside the Belfast platform in the direction of Miss Lynn's shop. The stable was located in a dip, which was quite deep, and fell away towards the Knock River.*

Wesley Thompson of the East Belfast Historical Society kindly passed me some research which had been carried out on the Knock Road by John Auld. This noted that there had been a plan to build a connecting avenue on flatter ground from King's Park to Cherryvalley, although this never actually transpired.

Taken from a point on Cherryvalley close to Orchard House Nursing Home and looking in the direction of Gilnahirk Road, in August 2007. The flooding at lunchtime on Tuesday 12th June 2007 resulted in subsidence of the road surface into the Knock River, which is located to the left. The road has been closed while repairs are underway.

(Courtesy of Linenhall Library from Belfast News-Letter)

On 29th November 1954 the Belfast News-Letter reported that 'residents of Summerhill spend their Saturday afternoon building a sandbag chain as a defence against the Knock River which caused serious flooding last week'. The 1902 Ordnance Survey map notes that just across the Upper Newtownards Road in the Stormont Demesne are the bold words 'Liable to Flooding'.

Apparently in years gone by the Knock River was inclined to flood (sounds familiar!) and in the early 1950's flooding had occurred on Barnett's Road to a depth of 5ft.

The builder who had levelled the ground was *'accused of blocking some drains from houses'*. It seems that the Ministry of Agriculture, Drainage Division was then responsible for all open rivers but some doubt existed about open rivers in urban areas. Later when the D.O.E. was established they cleared out the Knock River, and made steeper and more solid banks to prevent any re-occurrence. The Knock River rises in the Holywood Hills and is joined by many small tributaries which drain the surrounding area. Today many of these streams have been covered over or culverted, and only come to notice when localised flooding causes inconvenience or damage. The Gilnahirk River runs downhill behind the site of the old Tullycarnet School before meeting another stream at Kensington Road and the main Knock River at Cherryvalley alongside Cherryvalley Cottages.

Dermot Gallaugher: *Miss Lynn was a very astute businessperson and (I think) she held covenants preventing the opening of any other shops in the area. It was an excellent business and the nearest shop involved travel to Cherryvalley, the Upper Newtownards Road or Castlereagh. The shop also faced Brooklyn and after RUC headquarters opened in 1962 lots of policemen came in to buy newspapers and sweets. Miss Lynn built a more substantial retail premises on the site during the 1950's with an upstairs flat to replace the wee green hut. My Dad bought the business from her in 1959 when she retired, and Mum ran it until 1969 when it was sold. I remember working in the shop. We would open up at about 7.30 am each day to find local men, Jack Hinds and Tommy Heron, waiting to carry in the bundles of newspapers. They would stand and chat for a while before heading off up the Knock Road to do some gardening jobs.*

Behind Spokane there were a couple of very large houses in Cherryvalley. The next house to us was the home of Captain and Mrs Rutherford. When they went on holiday to the Slieve Donard Hotel, a notice would appear to that effect in the Belfast News Letter under the 'Court and Personal' column. So we took the opportunity to scamper around the lawns and peer in through the windows. The next house was the home of the Murphy family. Mr Murphy was Company Secretary for Harland & Wolff. A company car collected him each morning. I remember he always dressed like an undertaker. Dad died in 1963 at only 59 years of age, and after we sold Spokane in 1965, it was converted into a block of flats and subsequently demolished.

118

An aerial perspective of the Knock Road in 1970 and a great view of Brooklyn with the new RUC HQ extension at centre without walls or defences. Knockcastle Park has the look of a building site. Looking bottom left are Miss Lynn's new shop, then Cherryvalley and Spokane on the corner. To the right is an old outbuilding, part of Newmarket stables and next to the remains of Scott & Co's premises which are obscured by the trees beside the railway.

This photo was taken from just past Miss Lynn's shop and shows Knock Road in 1980. During the later road widening scheme half of Newmarket Lodge, 34 Knock Road had been demolished. This portion remains at the left centre of this view along with another old outbuilding (probably a stable) that is recorded on the Ordnance Survey map of 1920 although not listed as a dwelling in the Belfast Street Directory of the period.

Viola and husband Jacky Keenan enjoy a day out horse riding at Newmarket Lodge stable, 34 Knock Road in 1932. Knock Station was on the other side of the hedge.

(Courtesy of Frances Gibson by Alan Seaton)

A view of Knock Road in 1980 looking from the corner of Kensington Road towards Cherryvalley and Miss Lynn's wee shop with Ford Capri centre and Mark IV Cortina, left. Interesting to note the two old buildings further along on the same side of the road as the shop and the spire of Knock Methodist Church in the distance.

(Courtesy of Dermot Gallaugher)

Miss Lynn rebuilt her shop at 38 Knock Road in the late 1950's with an upstairs flat at 38a. Here is Sandra Gallaugher with her family in 1983. The corn and logwood mill marked on the 1858 Ordnance Survey map was very close to this site.

(The Belfast Street Directory for 1943 notes that the first residence on the right on entering Cherryvalley is called Woodlawn, now Cherrytree Walk and the occupier is Captain E.D. Rutherford, Surgeon, Royal Navy. Hugh Murphy JP occupies the next house, Cherrydene).

Dermot Gallaugher also recalls a frequent visitor to the shop during the 1950's and 1960's who was a larger than life character and lived not far away in Kensington Gardens.

Dermot Gallaugher: *In Kensington Gardens was Camlin's Nursery. Ernie Camlin was one of the sons of the owner and was known as 'The Ulster Frogman' or at least that is what he called himself. He would come into the shop and ask us to display signed photos of himself.*

The story of Camlin's Nursery has already been told in *Beaconsfield*. Ernest Camlin's family lived at Sydenham where he learned the horticulture business before going off to war service in 1914 with the 36th Ulster Division. On his return from active service he spent some time recovering from wounds in a military hospital. By 1922 he is listed in the Belfast Street Directory as E. Camlin, proprietor, Kingsden Park Nurseries, Kensington Gardens. He had signed the lease for the nursery land on 25th November 1920 from Jane Vahey (Herbert Vahey was listed as householder of Dovedale, 70 Knock Road in 1903) at a rent of 1d per annum eventually rising to £33 pa. The business traded at Knock until 1960.

The Court and Personal section of a local newspaper on 19th October 1951 reported that: *Their Excellencies the Governor and the Countess Granville accompanied by Lady Mary Leveson Gower this afternoon visited the nursery garden of Mr & Mrs Ernest Camlin, Kensington Gardens, Belfast.*

A later edition provided more detail on the story: *Three new carnations were christened yesterday by their namesakes the Earl and Countess Granville and Lady Mary Leveson-Gower. The Earl Granville is a deep rose; the Countess Granville is a glowing red and the Lady Mary a bright pink. All the carnations have proved their ability to stand firm and colour-true in this difficult world and are ready to face the public. The flowers were christened where they were born – in Camlin's Nursery at Knock, a place Her Excellency an enthusiastic gardener, has been anxious to visit since she saw a display of their flowers at an exhibition recently*

(Courtesy of Betty Jackson)

The Governor of Northern Ireland, Earl Granville and the Countess Granville (a sister of the Queen Mother) visit Camlin's Nursery at Knock in 1951 to inspect carnations named in their honour. Ernest Camlin, right with sons Davvie, centre and Ernie at rear.

This year marks the silver jubilee of the firms association with carnation growing. The Countess admired specimens of the Michael Shane Camlin carnation (which had been on the market for some time previously) in a long greenhouse that contained no fewer than 32,000 plants.

There were 3½ acres of glass in total and several members of Ernest's family worked in the business at various times including daughters Betty (Jackson), Sybil, Esme and Eileen, plus sons Davvie, Jack and Ernie 'The Ulster Frogman'.

Ernie Camlin was born in 1915. In later life he worked as a photographer and journalist and kept a number of scrapbooks, which recorded his various interests and exploits. He was by any standards an interesting and newsworthy character. He was educated at Methodist College and became a member of the Royal Horticultural Society when he went into the family business. He was an Associate of the London College of Music and a well-known figure on the concert platform with the Ulster Operatic Society as well as a life-long member of Collegians Rugby Club. He was a good enough player to be selected for the British Air Force of Occupation in Germany and played many matches for the RAF during the years 1940-46.

Ernie had joined the RAF in 1940, and served with the Casualty Air Evacuation Service. He also served at Castle Archdale, Co Fermanagh as well as in Holland and Germany and was an onlooker when tank flame-throwers burned the infamous Belsen Concentration Camp to the ground. He was stationed in the Hebrides and it was here he noticed Royal Navy frogmen at work, and after the war, that civilians in the south of France were turning underwater activities into a sport. (Jacques Cousteau had pioneered the 'aqualung' and made it popular). When Ernie returned to 'civvy-street' after being demobbed he thought of becoming the 'Ulster Frogman'. He bought his underwater equipment for £100 in 1954. The first job was to retrieve a model yacht, which sank in 30ft of water in the lower pond of Belfast Waterworks.

 In a local magazine article Ernie explained: *I will never forget Brussels four days after the liberation. There I was on a rough wooden platform in Belgium singing lustily of the 'Mountains of Mourne' and Paddy Reilly while hundreds of Belgians cheered themselves hoarse.*

(Courtesy of Betty Jackson)

Left, Camlin's advert shows that they were based at Kensington Gardens and Newtownards. This view from (what is now) Kensington Gardens shows the houses in the background which face Knock Road and are from right, Dovedale (later Kingsden) at 70 Knock Road then Dynevor, 72 Knock Road (both now demolished) and far left, 1 Kingsden Park which remains.

A higher profile was gained in Dublin during Easter 1956 when Ernie attempted to recover the 'An Tostal' flame, which had been thrown into the River Liffey by a student. A newspaper report carried the full story: *The An Tostal bowl of light on O'Connell Bridge Dublin, which disappeared into the Liffey during the early hours of April 19ᵗʰ 1953, by the hand of a medical student (who afterwards was prosecuted and had to pay for it) created long traffic queues. Last week Belfast frogman, Ernest Camlin made numerous dives to recover the flame.*

Later the same year Ernie had an eye for publicity at the Regent Cinema in Belfast during the Northern Ireland premiere of the Columbia film 'Cockleshell Heroes', which was attended by Prime Minister Lord Brookeborough. A local newspaper article explained the excitement of the occasion:

When the Prime Minister arrived at the Regent Cinema a fitting reception in the form of a Sea Cadet guard of honour had been arranged. He complimented their officers Lieut. J. Mallon and Lieut. L.Hutton on the smartness of their turnout on parade. The new film shows one of the strangest episodes of the war with graphic reality. Yet another masterpiece production of a story of heroic British fighters, tells how a small band of Royal Marines in tiny canoes paddled into Bordeaux harbour to destroy Nazi shipping. It stars Trevor Howard and Jose Ferrer and the film is in Cinemascope. Lady Brookeborough, Commodore Shillington, Commander Henderson, Air Commodore Hayes, Dr Dennis Rebbeck and the Minister of Home Affairs accompanied the Prime Minister who had a word of praise for the neat cadets and he also spoke to members of the Royal Marine Association.

Ernie Camlin was interviewed in 1970 for a magazine article and he spoke frankly about the business of gaining publicity through the media: *I went out and bought a Rolleiflex camera and carried it about with me everywhere. When you get your scoops, turn in the film with the captions, and you will find the newspaper does the rest. When on a diving job I would set up the camera with the correct aperture and get anyone to press the shutter. Thus I was in a position to offer exclusives to editors, and give my exploits blanket coverage. So if you want excitement with your newspaper articles, do what I did and become a frogman and dive for gold.* Camlin's Nursery ceased trading at Knock in 1960, although continued in business at Newtownards for some years, and it is now the site of residential housing at Kensington Gardens and Kensington Gardens West.

(Courtesy of Betty Jackson)

At the premier of war adventure film 'Cockleshell Heroes' in 1956, Ernie Camlin meets Northern Ireland Prime Minister Lord Brookeborough.

Passadena and Casiana
50 – 52 Knock Road and 2 – 4 Kensington Road

(Courtesy of Dermot Gallaugher and Margaret Henderson)

A new house: 2 Passadena, Kensington Road, home of J. M. Haig as it was in 1910.

(Courtesy of Tom and Anne McGuigan)

4 Passadena as it looked in 1998. The McGuigan's were the last family to live in the house before it was demolished to make way for the Kensington Crescent apartment block.

(Courtesy of Tom and Anne McGuigan)

The McGuigans had left 4 Passadena by Autumn 1998 when this picture was taken and the builders have already stripped the slates from the roof before demolishing the remains.

Tom and Anne McGuigan and family were the last residents of 4 Kensington Road – originally known as 4 Passadena. In 1983 the Chapman family had sold the property to the Adairs and they lived there for 11 years before selling to the McGuigan family in 1994. In 1998 Numbers 2 and 4 Kensington Road were then sold by Public Auction and the properties subsequently demolished later in the year, to make way for the building of the Kensington Crescent apartments.

The house lease contains some very interesting information on the ownership history of the site. It seems that Thomas McClure (mentioned in an earlier chapter) leased the 'parcel of land containing four acres and twelve perches' that included the Passadena site on the 5th July 1860 to Alexander Dickson (also mentioned in an earlier chapter) for the term of 10,000 years (a very far-sighted view!). The lease also describes the adjoining house as 3 Passadena and the wall and hedges between the premises as 'party wall and hedges'. The next door neighbour in Kensington Road in later years was Mr C.E. Burke (probably local retailer Mr C.E.Bourke) and the neighbour on the east side at Woodlawn (now the site of Cherrytree Walk) was linen merchant R.B.Park, later the home of Captain Rutherford. The premises were situated in the 'Barony of Castlereagh Lower, formerly County of Down but now County of the City of Belfast'.

In 1910 when J. M. Haig occupied 2 Passadena, all four semi-detached houses were known by the address of 1 – 4, Passadena, Kensington Road, Knock. In fact there were numerous name and number changes over the years. The earliest records for Passadena are in the Belfast Street Directory of 1905 when it looks like the houses are in the process of completion as numbers 1 and 4 are vacant, 2 has been occupied by J. M. Haig and 3 is in the name of G. McIldowie. The 1902 Belfast Street Directory lists 1-3 Kingston Cottages on the Passadena site and the 1903 Ordnance Survey Map shows a terrace of three small dwellings next door to Palermo.

In 1907 Robert Ponsonby Staples, Artist has taken up residence at 4 Passadena. An earlier address for Staples in the Knock area was simply Ashvale, Knock though it is not clear where this was located. By 1909 the family had moved to Bonchester on the Sandown Road next door to a large house called Dun Alastair (home of Alex Martin) near to the junction with King's Road. Robert Ponsonby Staples, third son of Sir Nathaniel Staples, 9th Baronet was born in 1853 at Lissan house, Cookstown, County Tyrone. After leaving the army, his father spent a number of years on the Continent, and his children received most of their education there.

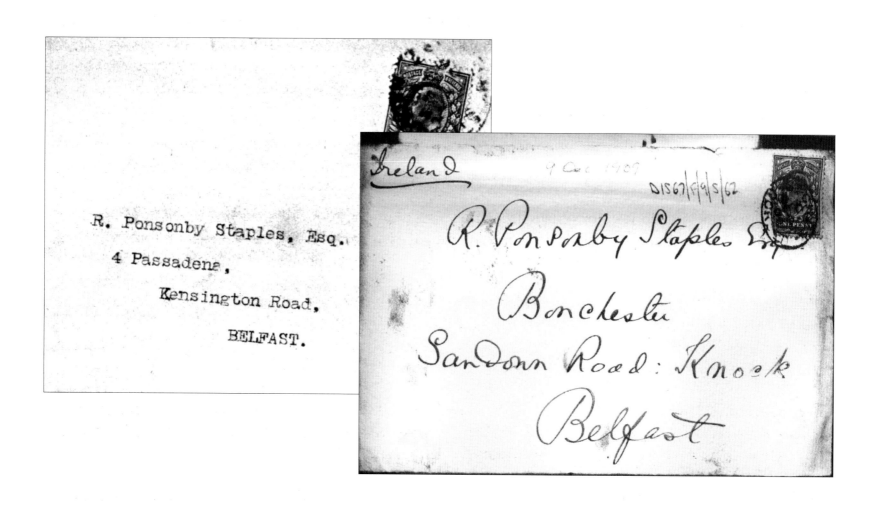

R. Ponsonby Staples, Esq.

4 Passadena,

Kensington Road,

BELFAST.

Ireland

R. Ponsonby Staples

Bonchester

Sandown Road: Knock

Belfast

(Courtesy of Deputy Keeper of the Records, Public Record Office of Northern Ireland from D1567/F/9/5/52 & 62)

Left is a letter to 4 Passadena, Kensington Road dated 6th April 1908. Robert Staples moved house to nearby Sandown Road and right on 9th December 1909 a letter is addressed to him at Bonchester, next door to Dun Alastair not far from the King's Road.

Staples studied art and architecture from the age of 12 and he taught art in London from 1897. His many works includes a triptych illustrating shipbuilding in Belfast and he also drew political cartoons.

As well as the grand sweep of a lifetime there is also the small print. Robert Ponsonby Staples was a great letter writer and the Public Record Office of Northern Ireland keep a file of his personal correspondence. It seems he had to work very hard to sell his art to the great and the good to gain patronage and make a living.

A recent BBC television programme on Belfast City Hall included a feature by Dr. Joseph McBrinn of the University of Ulster. It seems that in 1906 the plan for the interior of the City Hall was to reflect the grand thinking of the time, which was for ornate decoration with plasterwork, marble, stained glass and pictures. A series of murals was commissioned from Robert Ponsonby Staples to document the shipbuilding and linen industries – although this was never actually put on display.

Unfortunately for Staples in 1907 Belfast experienced the dockers strike and a period of civil unrest so Belfast Corporation took cold feet over the images depicted. They were uneasy about putting pictures of dockworkers on display in the City Hall after the protracted nature of the strike and the resulting ill-will between the workers and the owners. Apparently the triptych was tucked away in the Ulster Museum never to see the light of day.

Robert Ponsonby Staples had many unusual ideas about life, one of which was that the ills of modern life were a result of man's foolishness in insulating his body against the earth's magnetism by covering his feet in leather. He used to walk barefoot, hence his nickname 'The Barefoot Baronet'.

In politics, he was a Protestant Home Ruler and a member of the United Irish League. He carried his pad and pencil everywhere and was constantly sketching people and events of Edwardian life.

He played an increasing part in the running of the family estate in Lissane, Cookstown from 1905. He took up residence there in 1910 although he did not actually succeed to the property and the baronetcy until his elder brother died in 1933. He died in 1943.

Staples had written a letter to the Belfast Lord Mayor James Henderson on 15th May 1905 in which he is looking for work and proposes the idea of the triptych:

Dear Sir,

In view of the recent discussion on Art in the House of Commons... I submit the following offer to promote Art in Belfast.

Belfast has a new Town Hall...it is a great commercial centre and one of the chief industries is shipbuilding ...I have lately painted a picture of Harland and Wolff's yards.

I hereby offer to execute this work on a decorative scale, say about 15 feet long by 8 feet high for the Town Hall, provided the bare expenses of carrying out this work and the minimum remuneration for my time are provided. It would take about 50 working weeks if I were enabled to paint it in the Town Hall and the expense would not exceed £200.

I am not inexperienced in large undertakings.........

(Courtesy of Deputy Keeper of the Records, Public Record Office of Northern Ireland from D1567/F/9/5/3)

To put the figure of £200 into context, earlier in our story when John Archer was appointed Managing Clerk for Belfast Corporation, coincidentally in 1906, his annual salary was £200.

It seems that the whole project ran into some delay over Staples request to use a room in the 'New City Hall' as a studio and this gave rise to another letter to the Corporation on 14th December 1905.

To: Councillor McCartney, Chairman of the Improvement Committee, Town Hall, Belfast.

Sir,

In reference to my former letter asking the favour of the use of a room in the New City Hall to execute the Decorative Triptych, the design of which is now completed, I should be extremely obliged if your committee would consider the matter further.

The Royal Insurance Company inform me that using fires and lamps…would not in any way affect the insurances of the building.

I understood that this question of insurance stood in the way of your granting me the facility I required.

(Courtesy of Deputy Keeper of the Records, Public Record Office of Northern Ireland from from D1567/F/9/5/26)

There is a photograph of Staples (though not in this book) dated 1905 when working on the triptych at his studio in 4 Passadena. So it looks like his request to use a room in the New City Hall was never approved by the Corporation.

Staples also corresponded with a Mr Browne on 14th June 1906 when he was living at Knock and touches on matters of a family nature:

My Dear Browne,

My wife is keeping well only she is very bothered trying to drill Irish servants into more cleanly ways.

The children are exceedingly healthy. Violet gets two riding lessons a week from a job master whose stables are 300 yards from our house (Clegg's Newmarket Lodge?) – this is an antidote to bicycle riding the art of which she has picked up surreptitiously from her school friends. She has been worrying me for a cycle for at least two months.

Bob is doing very well at *Campbell College and is I believe eighth or tenth in a class of 30 boys where all or most of them are 2 or 3 years older than himself.I must stop now and let my typewriter get on with her other work as we are sending out from 500 to 1000 circulars about my work here.

(Courtesy of Deputy Keeper of the Records, Public Record Office of Northern Ireland from from D1567/F/9/5/41)

*Bob Staples was born in 1894 and left Campbell College in 1911. He served as a Lieutenant with the Army Service Corps during the Great War and eventually became Sales Manager with fridge maker Kelvinator Ltd.

Robert Ponsonby Staples, the 'Barefoot Baronet'. Notice he is not wearing any shoes.

By the 1950's the Chapman family had taken up residence at 4 Passadena although the name and address of the house had changed again. Susan Wilson (nee Chapman) takes up the story:

Susan Wilson: *We moved to 4 Kensington Road and the house name was Melfort. Next door at 2 Kensington Road was the home of Dr Fleming Fulton. We were semi-detached and on the left as you came into Kensington Road. There was another semi-detached next door although it was on the corner at 50-52 Knock Road.*

I went to school at Ashleigh House in Windsor Avenue off the Malone Road, and my brother Colin went to Campbell College, and then Inst. We went by bicycle in good weather, and the route we took went along the Hillfoot Road before the Knock dual carriageway was built. We turned into Cregagh Road and across to the Ormeau Road, and into Sunnyside Street to get to Windsor Avenue. There were very few cars on the roads in those days. My father had started his medical practice at the top of the Cregagh Road beside Cregagh Park, and my brother Colin is a GP continuing to practice at 372 Cregagh Road.

The entrance to Melfort is now the entrance gate to Kensington Crescent apartments. I also remember the gate lodge at Beaconsfield and the old man and woman who lived there for many years. When they died the place went to ruin. As a child I used to play in the gardens at Beaconsfield, and I vaguely remember the old woman who lived there. However we were only children at the time, and we ran around the gardens. We were frightened of her but after a while we got to know her and talked to her. I do remember Miss Crawford kept to herself and did not bother with people very much. All I can really remember is her grey hair. The gardens of Beaconsfield were always absolutely beautiful but as the years wore on, it became very run down. It was like a mini forest with lots of trees, and I remember the Weeping Willow tree in the Marie Curie courtyard long before the Centre was built.

The next house on Kensington Road from Melfort was called Kensington House and was the home of the Bourkes. They had a great shop on the Newtownards Road. I remember Mrs Bourke driving a Roll Royce. The house was gorgeous with great gardens, and it had an orchard attached and the driveway was directly opposite the Marie Curie entrance. We used to climb over the fence and steal the apples. It is now the site of apartments called Kensington Court and Kensington Gate.

Melfort had a cooker a bit like an Aga with coal-fired radiators before we changed to oil. We had the old bells in the house, which were used to call for maids or servants and there were also big wide fireplaces. There were 6 bedrooms and 3 bathrooms. We also had an air-raid shelter in our back garden for many years. When they tried to demolish it the handyman took forever to get the shelter removed and then gave up on demolition and just filled it in. I remember the construction of the Marie Curie Centre. We had nowhere to play because they fenced off the building site. We used to bring magazines for the patients to read. The matron in those days was Jean Harper. She went to school with my mother at Ashleigh House School. We left Melfort in 1983 and sold the house for £47,000. They eventually demolished the building in to build Kensington Crescent apartments.

Before Dr Chapman began his surgery in the late 1940's at 372 Cregagh Road the address had been 390 Cregagh Road and the house named 'Rubicon'. In 1941 the resident of No.390 was Mrs A. P. McFadzean, most likely the mother of William McFadzean VC.

(Courtesy left, William McFadzean website)

Left , Willam McFadzean VC and right his home 'Rubicon' at 372 Cregagh Road, now a GP Surgery. William's father (also called William) was presented with his son's VC medal by King George V at Buckingham Palace on Saturday 28th February 1917 having been granted a 3rd class return ticket from Cregagh to London.

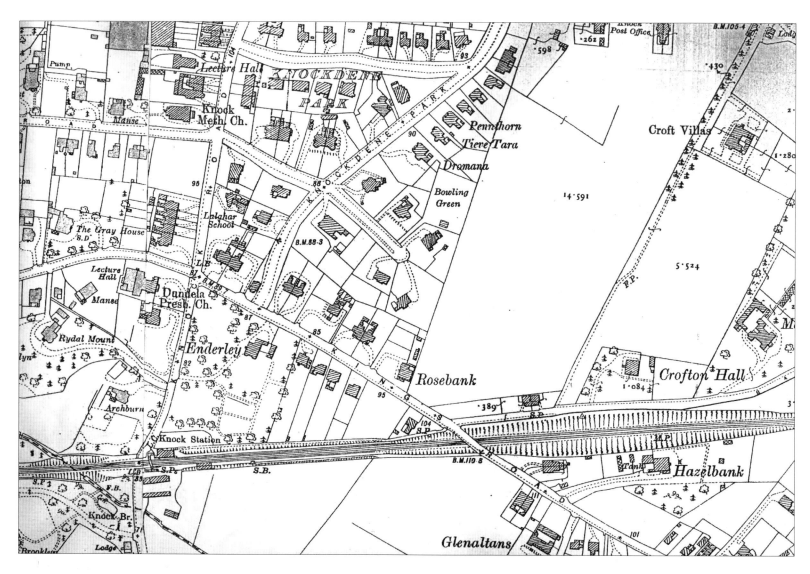

(Reproduced from the 1920 Ordnance Survey of Northern Ireland map)

The Knock Road runs left from the top of the page at Knockdene to Knock Station.

Enderly
8 Knock Road

Enderly as viewed from Knock Road. The house to the far right is 59 King's Road

Enderly first appears in the Belfast Street Directory in 1887 under Knock Village when the resident was Edward Emerson, J.P., commission agent, and the County Down Name Book for 1902 locates it as: *....a villa residence situated on the south side of the Kings Road, 7 chains (150 yards) North-North East of Knock Station. The property of, the Baroness Clanmorris, Bangor Castle, Co Down.*

Interesting to note that the first resident of Enderly was Edward Emerson. The last recorded resident in the 1950 Belfast Street Directory was Mrs Emerson so it looks like the same family had occupied the house throughout its lifetime as a family home. By 1959 the address at 8 Knock Road is described as vacant and the site has been re-assigned to 57 King's Road under name of Towell Trust – Old People's Home.

In fact an official invitation to the special occasion had been sent out by the directors of the Towell Building Trust to the special occasion of the opening of Towell House to be held on Thursday 2nd October 1958 at 3.00pm. Her Excellency the Lady Wakehurst carried out the opening ceremony with dedication by the Rt. Rev. W. McAdam M.A., D.D., Moderator of the General Assembley. The centrepiece of the opening ceremony was to be an unveiling of a tablet, expressing appreciation of the generosity of Mr David Towell, London who donated the funds for the building, by his niece Miss Betty Murphy, Bangor.

The early official literature of The Towell Building Trust states that it exists for: *The purpose of providing residential accommodation for people of advanced years and limited means, who are unable to maintain homes of their own.*

Mrs Fair who was a member of the committee wrote a brief history of Towell House in February 1991. Her husband had been Committee Chairman and the qualified surveyor who looked after the building programme.

Mrs Fair: Years ago, about 1949, Dr William Corkey was then Moderator of the Presbyterian Church in Ireland. When going around various Churches during his year he was moved with compassion for Ministers' dependants. A minister may be ill, and have to give up his Church and home, what is he do? Dr Corkey heard how the Church of Scotland had opened a couple of homes for elderly people. He went over to see them, came back and told ministers in the Church and prominent business men how much we needed the same thing.

So, a committee was organised, which started Adelaide House at the Malone area of Belfast. This was the beginning of the Presbyterian Residential Trust.

Very often we read in our daily papers how generous Northern Ireland people are in giving and indeed the Presbyterian Residential Trust can confirm that a committee was formed. My husband was the first chairman and he looked after the building of Towell House. As I too was on the committee I looked after the furnishings. A caretaker occupied the house while the building was erected, and it took two years to complete. The older building (Enderly) was made into a flat for the Matron and a nursing bay for the sick and the office and cloakroom were downstairs.

Lady Wakehurst opened Towell House in October 1958. She was the wife of the Governor of Northern Ireland. Mr Jack Andrews, Prime Minister of Northern Ireland took the chair. It was a successful day with a lot of rain!

On 3rd November 1960 Mr Towell died.

Mr Towell was born at Donaghcloney, Co Down in March 1872. After receiving business training in Lurgan he proceeded to London, whereby, with careful attention to business and strict integrity, he became a successful tailor. After his retirement from business in 1946, he and his wife took a deep interest in social work, and gave generously to Dr Barnardo's Home for needy children.

They were also very much interested in providing homes for elderly persons of limited means. Before his wife's death they had jointly decide to erect such a home for elderly people in Northern Ireland. It was through his generous benefactions that Towell House was erected. In the closing years of his life he was greatly interested in all that was being done in Towell House and often spoke of the joy it had given him to be associated with such work.

Towell House has been extended over the years and there is none of the Enderly building remaining today. In 2008 it will celebrate its 50th birthday.

This view of Enderly on the left provides a contrast with the modern look of Towell House and was taken from the old railway station on the Knock Road. There seems to be some debris in the garden of Enderly, which suggests the picture may have been taken in 1958 when Towell House was completed and officially opened .

This 1970 aerial view of Knock Road and King's Road junction is taken from above Knockdene. At bottom left, the large white house with tall chimneys is located at 86 & 88 King's Road (demolished) and was originally known as 'Maples' and 'Cedars.' Notice also the large house at 51 Knock Road (demolished) in the front grounds of Knock Presbyterian Church and the house in the grounds of Towell House at 32 Knock Road (demolished). Further along towards Brooklyn the white house is Archburn, 55 Knock Road and home of singer James Johnston.

(Courtesy of Derek Macafee)

A view of Dundela Presbyterian Sunday school in the late 1890's. There is no record of the names of the group although amongst the sitters is May Eve Aiken b.1890. The picture was taken in the garden of 86 King's Road. In the left background of this Autumnal scene is Dundela Presbyterian Church and to the right the end terrace at 49 Knock Road. Look closely to see a tower protruding from the roof of No.49 and although the house survives the tower does not.

There are not many clues as to when this photograph of Knock Presbyterian Church along with 51 Knock Road was taken. To the far left of the view a very close look reveals a metal archway with the bold words 'Dundela Presbyterian Church'. This confirms a pre-1921 vintage. Built in 1875, the foundation stone was laid by Sir Thomas McClure. Originally known as Knock, the name was changed to Dundela in 1875 and reverted back to Knock Presbyterian in 1921.

Archburn
55 Knock Road

Archburn Villa makes an appearance in the Village Directory of 1868 when the householder was John Shaw. The County Down Name Book for 1902 locates it as: *a villa residence situated off the Knock Road, 4 chains (90 yards) south east of Rydal Mount,* (now 53 Knock Road and also mentioned in the 1868 Village Directory).

The Gallaughers (of Spokane) bought Miss Lynn's shop in 1959 and ran it for the next 10 years and Dermot Gallaugher got to know the residents of the Knock Road very well : *On the other side of Brooklyn, heading towards King's Road was 57 Knock Road. The house was called Carrowshane. It had a gate lodge and a lovely garden. I can't remember who lived there. Next, the former opera singer James Johnston owned 55 Knock Road. When he left Covent Garden he ran a butcher's shop in Sandy Row. Jack Hinds was his gardener and they used blood from the shop to encourage plant growth - sometimes too vigorously! Then number 53 is Rydal Mount, which had a back entrance onto King's Road (identified as 49 King's Road) where the Boyd family lived. Next, 51 Knock Road, where the Kilpatricks lived, was called Closeburn. It was demolished some years ago and now forms part of the grounds of Knock Presbyterian Church . Then we come to the church and on the other side of King's Road was number 49, which is now an apartment block.*

The Ulster Family History Society website tells the official history of James Johnston:

James Johnston was born 17 August 1903, son of a Belfast butcher, who left school to work in his father's shop in York Street. He started singing in the Church choir, and, although he had no formal musical training, he won many baritone competitions until he was discovered to be a tenor. Thereafter he was in demand throughout Ireland and in 1932 he sang at the Eucharistic Congress. In 1945 Tyrone Gutherie offered Johnston a leading role and hewas Britain's leading tenor from 1945 until 1958. He was described by Lord Harewood as the singer to whom post-war British opera owes a great debt and he was noted for his big Italian roles. His singing of Nessun Dorma was often interrupted by applause. James Johnston said that he would quit while he was still at the top. His final performance at Covent Garden was in a production of Carmen in 1958. After that he returned to his Belfast butcher's shop in Sandy Row and he died on 17 October 1991.

Lalghar
6 Knock Road

The name of Lalghar first appears in the 1898 Belfast Street Directory and it is described as Knock Ladies School occupied by 'The Misses Beatty.' By 1901 it was listed as Knock Intermediate School and Kindergarten – Principal Miss Wylie. Although Lalghar is described as a girl's school it admitted boys in later years, as we shall see. In the 1902 Ordnance Survey Name Book it is described as follows.

Various modes of Spelling	Authority for modes of Spelling	Descriptive Remarks, or other General Observations which may be considered of Interest.
Lalghar School (New Name)	Miss Janis Wylie Lalghar School, Knock	Applies to a building used as an Intermideaite School for girls. Situated on the South side of Knock Road about 5 chains (100 yards) south east of the Methodist Church. This lady is getting no grant from any body. The property of Miss Janis Wylie, Lalghar School

(Reproduced from the 1902 Ordnance Survey of Northern Ireland Name Book)

(Courtesy of Joy Hill)

A great view of Lalghar in the 1970's. It was listed in the Belfast Street Directory as a school until the late 1930's. Miss Leta Wylie continued to live in the house until the mid 1960's and in the 1980's it was demolished for road-widening. James Wylie entered Campbell College in 1899 with a home address of 'Lalghar, Knock'.

Earlier in our story of Knock Joy Hill (nee Brownlee) had told of her life at Rosemount during the 1940's. The Brownlee family then moved to 445 Upper Newtownards Road, next door to J. L. Stewart's house at 2 Knock Road and Joy moved away to Canada only to come full circle a few years later to live at Lalghar.

Joy Hill: I got married to Samuel Grange Duckworth Hill in December 1954 and soon afterwards we moved to Canada to live. We really enjoyed Canada so we stayed for about 12 years and made some great friends with who I still keep in touch. We came back to Belfast in 1967, and after 2 years we noticed a large house called Lalghar at 6 Knock Road up for sale for at £6,500. Previously Lalghar had been a school and apparently Lalghar is a Welsh word, which means Red House, which of course it was. The main house had an extension to the side with the school building attached – which I think was an assembly room. There was no access from the house and both buildings had their own entrances. Lalghar's address was 6 Knock Road and the annex was 6a. When we bought the house Miss Wylie and her sister had already died. I think the house had been left to her housekeeper and Brian Morton was the estate agent.

After we bought the house there was a society called the Q.E. Club which used to meet there. When we bought the house we thought we would ask them to leave but as they were not doing any harm we let them stay on. I think Q and E were the code letters for 2 areas of the Civil Defence or Air Raid Precaution known as Q District and E District. The gentlemen apparently kept up their friendships via the QE club by playing snooker and the whist card game in the old Lalghar assembly building. We bought the house in 1969 and stayed 11 years. Then one day we got the Vesting Order for the road–widening scheme in about 1980 in the middle of a strike. The vesting order was a bit of shock so we moved to Castlereagh, where we built a new house. The Knock Road had been widened on a few occasions, and, in fact, was widened just before we bought the house in 1969. At that time most of the front garden was taken away. They were vesting many of the houses on the left-hand side of the Knock Road and in fact I think Lalghar lay empty for years until the late 1980's before it was eventually demolished.

Joan Shields (nee Doherty) attended Lalghar School in the 1930's: *I was born on 20th September 1925 and my family came from Clifton Park Avenue to Cherryvalley when I was 3 years old. Our address was 34 Cherryvalley Gardens, and we lived there for a while, and then moved to 46 Cherryvalley Park.*

(Courtesy of Joan Shields)

Lalghar School at 6 Knock Road in 1933. Middle row, 5th from left is Joan Doherty (now Shields). Back row, 2nd right is Patrick English, son of VC winner Major W.J. English, and resident of 16 King's Road. The rooftops are houses are 29, 31 & 33 Knock Road. Lalghar along with Lissadel at 4, J. L. Stewart's house at 2 and 86 & 88 Kings Road at the corner of Knock Road facing Knock Presbyterian Church have all been demolished to allow for road widening.

I started at Lalghar primary and there were 40 pupils. I stayed there until I went to Strathearn School. My teacher at Lalghar was Miss McWilliams who was the head teacher. Miss Moore, another teacher, went to Knock Presbyterian Church. I remember one Sunday she came to church in a straw hat, which had the price ticket dangling at the back and this caused great amusement to her pupils. I know the Misses Wylie ran Lalghar and they were often referred to but I don't remember ever seeing them. There was a house at the left as you entered Lalghar. I presume that Miss Wylie lived there, but I am not sure. I remember the school had a tin roof and an old fashioned stove for heat and it was an unpretentious building. My mother used to walk with me about half the journey. Then I met up with some friends for the other half. My dog, Prince, sometimes came around to the school of his own accord, and sat in the cloakroom under the peg, where my coat was hanging.

(The Belfast Street Directory from 1901 until 1965 refers at various times to The Misses Wylie, Miss Janis Wylie, Miss Leta Wylie and Miss A Wylie)

Peggy Kearney lived at 6 Shandon Park in the 1920's and also went to Lalghar School:

Peggy Kearney: *I was born in 1916, a war baby. I was at Lalghar before Joan Shields and our classroom was in the main house. When the Second World War came along, part of the school was turned into a canteen, and many of us helped out with making sandwiches. When we first came to live in Belfast from Downpatrick where my father worked in the bank, I attended Princess Gardens School in University Street (before it was moved to Dunmurry), which has been converted into a hotel and restaurant. After living briefly in the University area we moved to live at 6 Shandon Park and I then went to Lalghar School.*

I remember the three Miss Wylies who ran Lalghar School. Miss Lita Wylie was not as conventional as the other two. She played golf at Knock Golf Club. Another sister was called Miss Annie. There was a younger teacher brought in, and we all liked her very much but I can't remember her name. My father used to walk to Knock Railway Station and get the train to work. Leslie Johnston lived next door to us at Shandon Park, and he worked in a bank as well, and also went by train. In the afternoons I would ride my bicycle to meet my father on the afternoon train. One day Leslie Johnston raised his hat to me and I thought "what a wonderful man!" – he was such a gentleman.

155

I gave a Beaconsfield talk and slideshow presentation to the North Down Family History Society at Bangor on 16th March 2006. Later in the year, I received a letter from Mrs Catriona Murray, who lives on the Isle of Skye. She had read a transcript of the talk and it brought back some memories of Knock. It transpires that Mrs Murray's mother Florrie McCaw, had left Belfast when she got married to live in Scotland, although she returned to visit over the years.

Catriona Murray: I found the report of your talk to the N.D.F.H.S. last March very interesting. I really felt my 'roots' because my mother F.E. (Florrie) McCaw (1890-1975) lived on Kensington Road, Knock in a house called 'Grianan' a hundred years ago. (Grianan was located at 116 Kensington Road not far from Cherryvalley Park)

My mother went to Lalghar in 1902 aged 12 years and I have a prize book (June 1906) from 'Knock Intermediate School and Kindergarten, Lalghar, Knock' when she was 16 years old. She became a pupil teacher and joined the Kindergarten staff until she married in 1919. The other names that I recognised from your book are S.D. Bell, Mrs S.D .Bell, Mr Robert Bell, Willie Bell and Marion Hogg. They all appear in the list of folk who came with presents on my first visit to Belfast when I was aged only 4 months. The McCaw grandparents moved from Grianan after the Great War to Atlantic Avenue. Their only son was killed at the Somme and he was only 20 years old. My mother was born at 259 Albertbridge Road, Belfast, but when I went to look for it in 1990, it had gone. I suppose maybe it was bombed during the Blitz.

Knock Intermediate School - - - and Kindergarten, Lalghar, Knock.

THIS PRIZE

WAS AWARDED TO

Miss Florrie McCaw First in English + Mathematics. Form IV.

J. Wylie. Principal.

June, 1906.

(Courtesy of Catriona Murray)

Lalghar Intermediate School and Kindergarten in 1906. Centre, Miss Janis Wylie, 2nd row from top far left, Miss Wylie and Florrie McCaw and far right another Miss Wylie.

A view of Knock Road taken from outside Knock Methodist Church in 1980. The building far left is Lissadel, 4 Knock Road and on the corner of Knockdene Park South the white house is 4a Knock Road. Next door the tall brick building is Lalghar and just beyond a glimpse of 86 King's Road – all demolished by 2007.

Lissadel
4 Knock Road

(Courtesy of Robert Thompson)

Left, Lissadel, 4 Knock Road in c.1990 and right in 2007 after demolition for road widening. It was built in 1907 and was the home of Dr Wallace for many years before becoming Knockdene Welfare Home.

Lissadel was situated on the Knock Road at the corner of Knockdene Park South and facing Knock Methodist Church. There is no mention of Lissadel in the 1903 Belfast Street Directory although by 1907 the resident is Mrs E Cooper. Knockdene is mentioned in the Ordnance Survey Co Down Name Book, 1902. The Baroness Clanmorris owned the land on which Knockdene was built, as well as the Enderly site, on the south side of the King's Road as far as Knock station. All these lands had been shaded as Ballycloughan Nursery in the 1858 Ordnance Survey Map.

Various modes of Spelling	Authority for modes of Spelling	Descriptive Remarks, or other General Observations which may be considered of Interest.
Knockdene Park	Mr George Compton Knockdene	A small building estate actuate in the district of Knock on the south side of the Upper Newtownards Road Property of the Baroness Clanmorris Bangor Castle, Co Down

(Reproduced from the 1902 Ordnance Survey of Northern Ireland Name Book)

Bill Morrison mentioned the history of Knockdene and Lissadel in his 1999 article for the East Belfast Historical Society Vol.3/4, 'Knockdene Park'. He explains the history of the site with reference to a 1978 publication by Honor Rudnitzky entitled 'The Careys' which was about one of Northern Ireland's most famous water colourists J.W. Carey who lived in Knockdene Park from 1906 to 1937.

Bill Morrison: *In 1978 you could say that Knockdene Park had changed very little over the years although things have changed a bit since then. What a loss it was in 1992 when all the fine houses of Knockdene (from 2-6) fronting the Knock Road were cleared to make way for a dual carriageway, who knows, may never now be built.*

Lalghar, built in 1896 will for many be fondly remembered as Knock Ladies School. This fine house with its distinctive red tiled roof is now lost forever. So too is the stylish symmetrical terrace of three houses (named, Dunavon, Lissadel and Glenart) which many remember facing Knock Methodist Church. Built just a few years later, this delightful architectural period piece saw out its last years with dignity as a respected home for the elderly

Knockdene had been part of the huge estate owned by the Ward family of Bangor Castle. In 1841 the unit of land we now recognise as Knockdene was sold as a parcel and became the site of a profitable nursery,(Ballycloughan Nursery) thriving on supplying fruit and vegetables to the ever-increasing numbers of people, drawn to live and work in the industrialised city of Belfast. Very much still open country, the nursery was sold in 1870 to William McLeish, who some years later built the first houses in Knockdene. William McLeish began the pattern of semi-detached developments along the southern boundary of the nursery lands fronting King's Road. King's Road was formerly the Gilnahirk Road but was renamed at the Coronation of King Edward VII. The Maples and The Cedars sited at the corner of the Knock Road and the old Gilnahirk Road were the first houses that McLeish erected. (The original name of Maples and Cedars was 'Mapleville' and this first appears in the Village Directory of 1880 when John McLeish and W.H. Hamilton were the occupiers of the two houses)

Knockdene itself was not yet ripe for development but McLeish had the foresight to ensure that the nursery lands were laid out with avenues and planted up in preparation for the development – the pathways through the nursery setting the line for future roads. J.W. Carey moved into his newly completed house (in 1906), which was erected on the triangular corner site at the junction of Knockdene Park and the north cross route now Knockdene Park South.

By 1900 16 houses had been completed at Knockdene, and the remainder of the Gilnahirk Road frontage had been built up including nearby house Alona, which was the home of the well-known local tea merchant S.D. Bell. For many years Knockdene was entered through gates, remaining private until after the Second World War. The final run of detached houses in the north-east corner of the site were completed by 1915 as was Knock Bowling Club and (in 2007) Knockdene remains virtually unchanged from Edwardian times.

The Maples and The Cedars at 86 & 88 King's Road pictured in 1970 were the first houses built by William McLeish at Knockdene in the 1870's on the site of Ballycloughan Nursery. Look closely at far left of photo for the roof of 51 Knockdene Park.

A view of 51 Knockdene Park at the corner with King's Road in 1990 just before demolition. The semi at 86-88 King's Road is barley visible to the far left of the photograph.

An interesting aside to our story is that local near-neighbour J.H. Haig who lived at Passadena on Knock Road and then crossed Upper Newtownards Road to live at Hawthorden Road, had paintings by both local artists J.W. Carey and Robert Ponsonby Staples listed within his collection of valuables which had been drawn up for insurance purposes in 1917.

J.L. Stewart lived at 2 Knock Road (now demolished) from 1951 until his death in 1969 at the age of 88 years. He had previously sold Stewarts Cash Stores to Canadian Garfield Weston in 1935.

(Courtesy of East Belfast Historical Society)

The Tramway staff outside 2 Knock Road, future home of J.L. Stewart, probably in the 1920's.

A more familiar view of the site of J.L. Stewart's house in 2006 with heavy traffic approaching the junction. Notice the gable end with chimneys at 19 Knockdene Park North in both photographs.

Epilogue

Things keep changing!

The Marie Curie Hospice, Belfast has changed a lot since it was opened in 1965 and Marie Curie Cancer Care will be 60 years old in 2008. Much of the content of this book has come from the memories of people who have lived in Knock and who kindly shared their stories and old photographs. It has not been possible to include every single story in entirety - maybe these will appear in a later publication.

At the time of writing in summer 2007 several people who helped out have since died.

Mr Alan Seaton formerly of Kilhorne Gardens was a keen local photographer and some of his work is included in the story.

Mrs Dibble was 97 years old when she recalled with great clarity her early married life in Belfast with her husband James who was a member of the Cherryvalley ARP.

Wilson Lewis remembered the crowd of people who visited their house to watch the Coronation on the first black and white television in Shandon Park.

Susan Wilson had fond childhood memories of Beaconsfield and Kensington Road

To get the best from this book – read it carefully then walk around Knock and identify all the places mentioned. I found this was great fun and so did my wife Christine.

Acknowledgements

It takes a long time to write a history book and all that is needed is plenty of time, a little persistence, relevant material and the support and co-operation of many people to help out. So I will thank them in the chronological order in which the research took place:

Tony Merrick was very generous with the Hurley family story and photographic archive of Knock during the writing of Beaconsfield and this time he provided me with some interesting additions to Fred Hurley's photos and other family history. Betty Jackson was a font of knowledge on Knock and particularly Camlin's Nursery.

Roy McConnell bought a copy of Beaconsfield and kindly contacted me with the McConnell and Fair Head stories – all archived and maintained with great care. Joan and Norman Shields are well informed about Knock. They pointed me in the direction of Lalghar School and Peggy Kearney who has excellent recall of the formation of Shandon Park Golf Club. On a Sunday afternoon, Cecil and Daphne Molyneaux and Margaret Scarisbrook looked out old photographs of Dundela and recalled family life on the Knock Road – which ties in nicely with Trevor Mercer and the beginnings of Hillmount Nursery. I met May Twist at Joymount Presbyterian Women's Association at a Beaconsfield talk which led to a couple of very interesting conversations with Stuart Twist and the discovery of the Cherryvalley ARP minute book. I am now much better informed on the need for stirrup pumps during an air raid.

Stuart then put me in contact with Maureen Dibble and her late mother Mrs Dibble for more information on the Cherryvalley ARP and Miss Archer of Owen Varra. At the Marie Curie Volunteers Christmas dinner I met Margaret Henderson who provided a super copy of an old photograph of Passadena which in turn made the connection with Dermot Gallaugher and Miss Lynn's wee shop. Dermot turned up some great old photo's and recalled Spokane and Gallaugher family life with great humour and insight. The late Susan Wilson also helped with her fond memories of Passadena and life as a teenager in the district. The Brooklyn story was helped greatly by the file on the old house kept at the Police Museum. Hugh Forrester, ably assisted by Harry turned up some wonderful aerial photographs of the area. Thanks also to Keith Thompson for old Brooklyn photographs.

Joy Hill clearly remembered Rosemount and the German POW's at Brooklyn as well as Lalghar School. Gary Allen was helpful on the origins of Towell House. Frances Gibson kindly met the late Mr Seaton in connection with his photograph collection and Wesley Thompson generously provided access to the John Auld photographic and written archive on Knock. Thanks also to Daphne Castles for making available some old photos from the collection of her late husband Charles Castles and to Derek Macafee for the old photo of Dundela Sunday School. Robin Heatly helped out with the old photograph of St Finnian's. Mrs Catriona Murray who has family origins in Kensington Road now lives on the Isle of Skye and had received the newssheet of the North Down Family History Society. This is turn has resulted in correspondence concerning the family history of the McCaw's and another link to Lalghar School. Thanks to the following local historians for their permission to reproduce materials: H.Crawford Miller, Mike Maybin, Billy Montgomery and Desmond Coakham. Thanks to Heather Stanley of the Public Record Office of Northern Ireland for permission to reproduce their materials, Drew Ferris of the Ordnance Survey of Northern Ireland for copies of old maps and also the Linenhall Library for old newspaper clippings. Also to Darwin Templeton, Editor of the News-Letter for kind permission to reproduce many old photographs from past editions.

Proof reading is an important part of this process and I never underestimate the power of a well placed comma or apostrophe. So special thanks for proof-reading to Rita Moore, Betty Martin and Honor Baird for your diligence and precision and to Rosalind Colledge who doubles as the Beaconsfield Sales Person. Almost finally to Janna Moore, Volunteer Services Manager at the Marie Curie Hospice for getting behind this project with 'a heart and a half' as you did with Beaconsfield previously to make it a resounding success – you never know, there might be another book in the not too distant future! Thanks also to Alec Barclay, Regional Fundraising Manager of Marie Curie Cancer Care.

To my wife Christine – thanks for lots of cups of tea and going on walking tours with a camera around Knock. I was not joking when I said there might be another book! A third book on the history of the greater Knock area is due for publication in 2009 and will be entitled 'Cherryvalley'. The scope of the story will include Cherryvalley (or as it was known in the 1800's 'Knock Village'), Shandon Park, Kensington Road, King's Road and Gilnahirk. I would not be here without my ancestors. So, with a sense of family history, here are some photographs of them too:

Left William (Billy) Wallker, married Henrietta Anderson centre, in 1922 and they had eight children including my mother Edith who would later marry my father Reverend Ernest (Multi) Campbell in 1956. Billy joined the Army Service Corps in 1915 aged 16 years and was at the battle of Ypres. He was a cousin of Harry Walker mentioned earlier in this story.

Right, Arthur Campbell and Sara Brett pose in 1903 after their wedding. They would have four children including my father Ernest (Multi) Campbell. Arthur was a Sergeant in the RIC and made the wise career move of marrying his boss's daughter.

Nuala Campbell left and twin brother Aidan Campbell, right (that's me) at The Vicarage, Glenavy in 1960. Nuala's car was stolen from our home at 51 Ballygomartin Road sometime in 1962 – anyone with information on the whereabouts of Nuala's car should immediately notify the police.

Marie Curie Hospice Belfast

Marie Curie Cancer Care was founded in 1948 and celebrates its 60th anniversary in 2008. Over the last 60 years, there have been many changes and developments in the services delivered to patients with life-limiting illnesses and their families.

At present the services offered in Northern Ireland are:

- 200 Marie Curie Nurses who care for people with life-limiting illnesses in their own homes across the province.
- 18 bedded in-patient unit with over 300 admissions per year.
- Day Therapy offered in Belfast, Newtownards, Lisburn and Downpatrick.
- Breathing Space – a weekly out-patient facility to assist patients with the management of breathlessness.
- Permanent in-house Palliative Care Medical Consultants
- Physiotherapy, Occupational and Complementary Therapies
- Patient and Family Support Team which includes Senior Social Workers, a Chaplain, and a specially trained group of Bereavement Support Volunteers.
- Educational Services and training support for Marie Curie staff and other healthcare professionals.
- Over 180 hospice volunteers, 100 shops volunteers and many more people throughout Northern Ireland who contribute to fundraising for Marie Curie.

The volunteers give their time and skills free of charge to provide a wide range of services such as driving patients to appointments, serving meals, gardening, helping in the kitchen, working on reception and many other wide and varied duties!

All the proceeds from the sale of this book go to Marie Curie Hospice, Belfast. Your support is gratefully received. Telephone the Marie Curie Hospice at 0280 90 882000 to either buy a copy of the book or arrange for a talk and slideshow at your group.

Thanks again.

Aidan Campbell , November 2007

Select Bibliography

I found that the following works by local historians have all helped to shape the Knock story and I am grateful for all their efforts and scholarship. I enjoyed these books over many evenings and I hope everybody has been duly acknowledged: Belfast Street and Ulster Village Directories. Ordnance Survey Maps and Name Book. The Ulster at Dundonald, CJH Logan. The Church on the Stye Brae, 1787-1987, HC Miller. Gilnahirk Primary School 50 Years 1939-1989. Belfast & County Down Railway, Desmond Coakham. Tramway Memories Berlfast, Desmond Coakham. Belfast's Lost Tramways, Mike Maybin. Ireland in the age of the Trolleybus 1938-1968, Mike Maybin. Snapshots of Belfast, Photographs of old Belfast 1920-1929. Wheels Around Ulster, BC Boyle. Belfast Corporation Buses, 1926-1973, WH Montgomery. Bombs on Belfast, The Blitz 1941, Introduction by Christopher D McGimpsey. Images of Ireland, East Belfast, Keith Haines. Buildings of Belfast 1700-1914, CEB Brett. The East Belfast Historical Society, various Journals. Old Ordnance Survey Maps, Alan Godfrey Maps, commentaries. The Knock, John Auld. Edwardian Belfast, a social profile, Sybil Gribbon. Written in Stone, Tom Hartley. The Hidden Famine in Belfast, C.Kinealy and G.MacAtasney. No Mean City, B.Walker and H.Dixon. Belfast, The Making of the City, J.C.Beckett. Ordnance Survey Memoirs of Ireland, Parishes of County Down, 1832-4, 1837. St.Finnian's Cregagh, 1932-1982, David Hammond. East Belfast, Keith Haines and Martin Cooke.

Front Cover Photograph:
A BCDR Belfast-bound train waiting at Knock Station in the 1930's with the King's Road bridge in the background.

Back Cover Photographs:
Top Right, Earl and Viscountess Granville examine Carnations at Camlin's Nursery, Knock in 1951.
Middle Right, George and Margaret Molyneaux at the front door of Dundela, 95 Knock Road in 1925.
Bottom Right, Pupils at Lalghar School, 8 Knock Road in 1933.
Bottom Centre, The Hurleys in 1883 at Cremorne Villas, Holywood Road, before moving to Beaconsfield.
Bottom Left, The Gallaugher family of Spokane, 48 Knock Road on a grand day out at Portrush in 1952.